T0328484

Khrushchev's Putsch

Khrushchev's Putsch

Reversing the Socialist Program
and
Wrecking the Soviet Union

GERHARD SCHNEHEN

Algora Publishing
New York

Library of Congress Cataloging-in-Publication Data

Names: Schnehen, Gerhard, 1949- author.
Title: Khrushchev's putsch : reversing the socialist program and wrecking
   the Soviet Union / Gerhard Schnehen.
Description: New York : Algora Publishing, [2020] | Includes
   bibliographical references. | Summary: "In a compact book built on
   quotes on primary sources, Schnehen shows that Khrushchev essentially
   pulled off a coup, eliminating Stalin and then Beria. This opened the
   future to a radical shift away from the policies that had enabled the
   Soviet Union to make the hair-raising jump into the modern
   industrialized world and pulled it through the devastating war.
   Khrushchev reversed major achievements and brought havoc to the Soviet
   economy and society"—Provided by publisher.
Identifiers: LCCN 2020040078 (print) | LCCN 2020040079 (ebook) | ISBN
   9781628944280 (trade paperback) | ISBN 9781628944297 (hardback) |
      ISBN   9781628944303 (pdf)
Subjects: LCSH: Khrushchev, Nikita Sergeevich, 1894-1971. | Beria, L. P.
   (Lavrentii Pavlovich), 1899-1953. | Stalin, Joseph, 1878-1953. | Soviet
   Union—History—1953-1985—Sources. | Soviet
   Union—History—1925-1953—Sources.
Classification: LCC DK275.K5 S43 2020 (print) | LCC DK275.K5 (ebook) |
   DDC 947.085/2—dc23
LC record available at https://lccn.loc.gov/2020040078
LC ebook record available at https://lccn.loc.gov/2020040079

Printed in the United States

Author's note

All quoted material from foreign languages, mostly German, have been translated into English by the author. I assume full responsibility for possible errors or inaccuracies.

TABLE OF CONTENTS

INTRODUCTION

"Beria is the most slandered and libeled politician in the history of the Soviet Union."[1]

This audacious statement by Prof. Grover C. Furr of Montclair University, a professional researcher on Soviet history, will serve as our starting point.

Indeed, an unbiased review of primary resources leads one to some rather shocking conclusions about how the history of the Soviet Union has been misrepresented. Slander and libel against Beria and Stalin have been repeated until they took on the sheen of accepted truth.

What they'd been fighting for was the rights of the working poor. This kind of agenda tends to draw the wrath of the elites, who, after Stalin's death in 1953, were quick to move things in a different direction.

While detesting these two, the West has always been sympathetic to Khrushchev. He was heralded for his "courage" in condemning his predecessor and for introducing capitalist

[1] Grover C. Furr, *Stalin and the Struggle for Democratic Reforms, Part Two*, p. 7, at: http://clogic.eserver.org/2005/furr2.html.

elements into the Soviet economy. In fact, he was put in place precisely to dismantle the socialist system, especially the socialist economic system, which had been created under Lenin and Stalin, and to substitute it with an essentially capitalist system ruled by the profit principle and a privileged nomenclature.

The facts, the actual record, show that Stalin and Beria fought to build socialism, prioritizing the interests of the workingman. But even the new Russian rulers are to some extent descendants of Khrushchev and are building a hybrid system with many capitalist features — although it must be said that President Putin stopped the pro-Western oligarchs and has put Russian interests first, to the dismay of the West.

After Stalin's violent death in 1953, Beria, the former Soviet Minister of the Interior and head of the NKVD (the forerunner of the KGB), officially became the number two in the official hierarchy of the Soviet state. In fact he was the most influential and active Soviet politician at that time. He fought to secure the primacy of working class interests, against all odds. A number of his accomplishments will be discussed shortly. But in the West as well as in much of Russian historiography, slander and libel against him are even today presented as irrefutable evidence of a vicious ill intent.

To take just one example of how Beria is depicted in today's official Russia, let's look at *Russiapedia*, presented by RT TV, which is publicly financed from the budget of the Russian Federation. The website mentions that Lavrenti P. Beria was born on March 29, 1899 and died on December 23, 1953. They correctly point out that Beria was no Russian; he was a Megrel from Abkhazia, and that he did not die a natural death. A few details to frame the rest of the rhetoric.[1]

Beria was executed after a military tribunal condemned him to death with six of his closest collaborators in Moscow in December 1953. They don't mention that only selected military personnel were allowed to follow the trial proceedings, which were closed to the general public. Beria's son Sergo in his book

---

[1] https://russiapedia.rt.com/prominent-russians/politics-and-society/
lavrentiy-beria/

on his father[1] even claims that his father did not get a trial at all but was shot months before the "trial" in late June of 1953 by a special unit, in his own house. The trial, he writes, was staged later in December using actors.

So, something which is highly contested and on which as yet no light has been shed is treated as a proven fact. But that is not all we learn about Beria. *Russiapedia* starts right out on a strong note:

> Lavrenti Pavlovich Beria was certainly one of the most vicious and mysterious figures of Stalin's era.

"Certainly." Where is the certainty, why are the authors so sure? If he was one of the "most mysterious figures" in Russian history, and if the many myths and legends have not been cleared up yet, how do the authors know that he was "one of the most vicious figures"?

Let's read a little further.

> Stalin rewarded Beria's dog-like loyalty by making him head of the NKVD. It is rumoured that Beria personally strangled his predecessor [Yezhov]. Stalin used Beria to stage his purges. Beria used this opportunity to murder as many old Bolsheviks as he could, thus eliminating as many of Stalin's political rivals as possible and going so far as to order the mass execution of several thousand political prisoners he had already sent to detention camps...

> Beria was viewed by many, including his own party comrades, as not just a distasteful monster, but as a vicious sexual predator. He reportedly kidnapped young girls on Moscow streets, raping and sodomizing them and threatening their families to keep quiet.

> Beria apparently attempted to use his position as chief of the secret police to succeed Stalin as sole dictator.

Rumored, reportedly, apparently. The authors openly admit that they are spreading rumors, but they can't help themselves. The temptation to do so must have been overwhelming. Why not repeat what has been said many times before, especially during the Khrushchev era, and which therefore must be true, at least

---

[1] Sergo Beria, *Beria, My Father. Inside Stalin's Kremlin*, London, 1999.

partially true? Why not mention such things on the official page of a TV channel that claims to inform its listeners and readers objectively and fairly, in contrast to Western media?

Beria himself was a Bolshevik all his life. He was a member of the Georgian and also of the Transcaucasian Communist Party; he worked for this party nearly all his life, and was even its leader at one time. Why should he have wanted to kill the comrades he depended upon? Why should he have been interested in diminishing the number of his collaborators? As no such motive existed, the authors claim that he did it because he had a "desire to kill."

But then, why did he free thousands of prisoners from labor camps and prisons after he took over from Yezhov as chief of the Soviet secret service NKVD in late 1938? He rehabilitated them in the thousands. It was he who ended the "Great Terror" in 1939, a horrific campaign launched by Yezhov and his group which claimed the lives of more than 700,000 people in the Soviet Union between 1937 and 1938.

Why did he champion a law, after Stalin's death, according to which more than a million camp and prison inmates were freed and given an amnesty, if he was such a despicable monster and serial killer?

In the end, the authors of the Beria entry probably felt that it would help to bring the piece to a close somewhere back in the realm of facts. They found this much to add:

> He was also known to be a good balalaika player and had
> a fast hand with a revolver.

This part is true, and rounds up the fact-count in the short biography. Congratulations, Russian journalists! You did an excellent job!

In the photo attached to the entry, Beria is seen with a great number of decorations hanging from his breast. If one takes a closer look at it, it turns out to be a photo montage apparently intended to suggest arrogance and flashiness. In his usual photos, Beria never wears more than one order, the one in the shape of a red star, the order of "Hero of Soviet Labor." In most cases he just wears a suit and a hat.

The *Russiapedia* also has a short "biography" (if you can call it that) of Nikita Khrushchev, the man who organized the plot against him, had him arrested in the midst of a politburo session, put him behind bars and later had him executed. During his eleven-year term in office as First Secretary of the Soviet Communist Party, Khrushchev more than once boasted of this feat of his, including in his memoirs. But he also saw to it that other Stalin loyalists lost their lives in the years 1953–1956, among them Vladimir G. Dekanozov, the former Soviet ambassador in Berlin appointed by Stalin and Molotov to deal with the Nazis before the war; and the former head of the Azerbaijani Communist Party, Mir D. A. Bagirov.

Here's what they write about Khrushchev:

> Khrushchev's leadership marked a dramatic change in the Soviet Union...The so-called "Khrushchev's Thaw" followed, meaning less political control and censorship, and more openness and a rise in living standards... Khrushchev was fond of reading and gardening.[1]

The incident at the United Nations in 1960 is, of course, also mentioned, when Khrushchev banged his shoe on the lectern during a speech he made. We do not find such human attributes in the description of the sadist and rapist Beria, who is still vilified up to this very day on certain "documentaries" on "YouTube." There Beria is abused in part also to discredit Stalin, who obviously trusted him.

Beria was also the man responsible for the building of the Soviet A-bomb, by the way. He oversaw the project launched in late 1945 to break the US monopoly on nuclear weapons after the US had used two nuclear bombs to destroy the Japanese cities Hiroshima and Nagasaki in August 1945.

In 1949, the first Soviet atom bomb was tested — to the dismay of the US imperialists. The authors seek to belittle Beria's achievement in this respect, writing that:

> The extraordinary success was achieved at a high price. Beria created a climate of total secrecy and immense fear within the project. Everyone involved was under constant surveillance at all times, even the top scientists.

---

[1] At: http://russiapedia.rt.com/prominent-russians/leaders/nikita khrushchev/.

The head of one department was sentenced to eight years in prison for reportedly boasting to his family about the work being conducted.[1]

No evidence is given to support the allegations made by Beria's adversaries taken at face value. For decades now, these stories have cropped up again and again in connection with Beria's name to make him appear to have been some sort of Soviet Gestapo leader.

At the same time, Khrushchev's infamous role as party chief in Ukraine is skillfully swept under the carpet — or the authors of *Russiapedia* have no knowledge of it. Khrushchev had more than 50,000 party members arrested and thousands murdered in Ukraine by a so-called *troika* he himself was a member of. All we hear about this is the following remark:

> He went to work in Ukraine, but was soon recalled to Moscow.[2]

This is completely untrue: He spent a full eleven years in the Ukraine (1938–1949), as party chief of the Ukrainian Communist Party, where he organized the great wave of repressions against ordinary party members with the support of Nikolai Yezhov, Chief of the NKVD, German spy, and a member of the Soviet opposition. Yezhov was executed in 1941 for high treason after a long trial proving that he had worked for German intelligence since 1934 and carried out the orders of the German military attaché in Moscow, General Koestring, who was linked to the German Gestapo. Khrushchev's friend Aleksandr I. Uspensky, whom he appointed chief of the Ukrainian NKVD when arriving in the Ukraine in 1938, was later executed for participation in Yezhov's anti-Soviet crimes. But Khrushchev, who had powerful protectors in the Soviet Central Committee, escaped punishment.

Nor is Khrushchev's earlier role as head of the Moscow party organization (in 1937) mentioned in Russiapedia. Khrushchev liquidated almost the whole leadership of the Moscow party organization, claiming that it was a nest of spies and of "enemies

---

[1] Ibid., Beria biography in RT's *Russiapedia*.
[2] Ibid., Khrushchev biography in RT's *Russiapedia*.

of the people." After he was dismissed and sent to the Ukraine, the repressions in Moscow ended under the new head Aleksandr S. Shcherbakov.

Khrushchev's amnesty of political prisoners is mentioned in RT's *Russiapedia*, but Beria's amnesty of 1953 is not — when he had more than a million prisoners and labor camp inmates released. And at the time when Beria and the Soviet Council of Ministers proposed this amnesty, Khrushchev was among those who voted against it, Prof. Grover Furr tells us in his book *Khrushchev Lied.*

So, the state-funded Russian TV channel RT gives a completely biased picture of Beria on the one hand and Khrushchev on the other. The latter seems more to their liking, or, to put it more bluntly: They simply adopt the old lies against Stalin and Beria that were spread by the Khrushchev, Brezhnev and Gorbachev regimes in the Soviet Union, and they even popularize them in their history section.

Another view of Beria is presented by Sputnik (formerly Voice of Russia), the Russian government's international radio broadcasting service. There we read about the events following Stalin's sudden death:

> On March 5, 1953, after the death of Joseph Stalin, the Soviet Union was left without a head of state. In the country a fierce battle for power started between the chairman of the Council of Ministers of the Soviet Union, Georgi Malenkov, the chief of the secret service, Lavrenti Beria, and the Secretary of the Central Committee of the CPSU, Nikita Khrushchev.
>
> After long debates, the political nomenclature, however, opted for Khrushchev, and on September 7, 1953, half a year after Stalin's death, he was elected First Secretary of the Communist Party of the Soviet Union.[1]

No word about violently eliminating and liquidating Beria along with six of his colleagues, all of them Georgians.

The event is completely ignored — or again, the authors know nothing about it, which seems to be the most likely variant. The reader is made to believe that there was the usual power

---

[1] http://sputniknews.com/german.ruvr.ru/radio_broadcast/4003214/85.

struggle after a political vacuum had emerged and that in the end Khrushchev was "elected." Who elected him? The nomenclature; but what exactly was this "nomenclature"? Who were the people who elected Khrushchev after the "debates"? Did any of these discussions take place at all? Then the articles praises Khrushchev for his "reforms" which allegedly led to "a rise in living standards" in the USSR.

So we must conclude that the official Russian historiography upheld by RT and Sputnik even now sticks to the old legends carefully cultivated over so many decades during the Khrushchev, Brezhnev and Gorbachev eras. They have never, at least officially, been questioned in open debate or allowed to be challenged, but are treated as established facts and truths. The events surrounding Beria's arrest, confinement, trial and violent death — like many other Bolsheviks in the early stages of Khrushchev's era — are almost always ignored and treated as non-events. No debate or discussion about the truthfulness of this sort of historiography seems to be possible in today's "democratic" Russia.

In view of this kind of "historiography" it is very difficult to look for what really happened during the aforesaid power struggle in 1953 and to put together a comprehensive and true picture. What was really going on and how did Khrushchev finally succeed in outmaneuvering his rivals? They stood for a completely different policy and orientation than he — the saboteur and destroyer of socialism — did.

The archives that were opened for everybody in the early 1990s were soon closed again (in 1996) to the general public, and only selected people and historians who supported the official version of events were allowed access. Why? Because dissident voices are not welcome. Those who are permitted to read the documents in the state archives are expected to write articles or books to defend the official school of thought, to make sure that nothing changes and that the old myths, fairy tales and legends of the winners of that power struggle (which was decisive for the future development and orientation of the Soviet Union) are upheld and can then enter the history books for the Russian school kids.

One of those who succeeded in getting access to the Russian archives is the author Vladimir Nekrassov, who wrote a disparaging book on Beria where he calls him "Stalin's butcher." He was not denied access, as he strictly abides by the official line. Nevertheless some interesting details can be found there, among them Marshal Zhukov's confession that he was the one who arrested Beria. Zhukov later denied that, when he had fallen out with the Khrushchevites. Nekrassov also tells us that prior to Beria's arrest, military exercises had taken place around Moscow, probably to make sure that Beria's own troops had no chance to intervene in the planned operation to oust him.

It is said that more than 40 volumes of documents and case files pertaining to Beria's trial are still under lock and key. During the Stalin era, reports of court proceedings were published to familiarize everybody with what was said and done during trials, except for those trials of a military character. Other socialist countries, such as Hungary, Bulgaria and Czechoslovakia, followed the example and published the reports of court proceedings of important political trials, among them the trial against Rudolf Slánský's conspiracy, the trial against Laszlo Rayk in Hungary and the one against Traicho Kostov in Bulgaria. There we find all the pertinent details on what was said by the accused or by the prosecutors and judges. The general public, even Western journalists and ambassadors, were invited to watch the proceedings.

But this sort of transparency was ended under the Khrushchev regime and the regimes he installed in Eastern Europe. The minutes of the crucial politburo session held in June 1953 have still not been released by the Russian Federation. This is when Beria, as Minister of the Interior, was said to have been arrested at gunpoint by a group of Soviet army officers, among them Georgi Zhukov and Kyrill Moskalenko. Meanwhile the speeches made by Beria's adversaries at the Central Committee Plenum the next month, while Beria was in custody, were made public. Thus, his accusers were given full voice while the arrested minister himself was deprived of any chance to make his point and to defend himself.

When Khrushchev made his infamous "Secret Speech" at the 20th Congress of the Communist Party in February 1956, most delegates were already on their way home. The speech was kept secret from the Soviet general public for years to come, but in

the West the speech was soon made available and widely publi-
cized!

Why this secretiveness up to the present day? Why not
release these old documents after so many years so that people
can study them and then reach their own conclusions on what
had happened? Someone, some group, in the present Russian
government is not prepared to open the archives on the Beria
trial. Obviously, they are afraid of the truth.

It is hard to tell if Putin is involved in this cover up. He is
working assiduously to uphold Russia's sovereignty, but at the
same time he needs the support of the new Russian bourgeoisie.
They would not accept a Socialist leader, and if he turned
socialist or even anti-Zionist one day, we can well imagine they
would remove him in a putsch "on health reasons." Putin never
mentions Stalin on the occasion of May 9th celebrations and he
never finds a good word to say about his great job during the
Nazi invasion; he once called him a "dictator and tyrant." His
opinion about Beria, I do not know

One possible reason for keeping the records secret would
suggest that Nikita Khrushchev introduced capitalist principles
into the Russian economy to undermine the socialist regime. The
present Russian government is anti-Socialist and pro-capitalist,
and on that score they are favorably disposed towards Khrushchev and also toward Gorbachev.

But an almost opposite conclusion may be a better explana-
tion:

Publishing the documents now could really open a can of
worms, as the chief culprit of the crimes was not Stalin but
Nikolai Yezhov, the former NKVD chief and Nazi spy who was
close to Khrushchev during the Great Terror in the late thirties.
Yezhov was tried in 1941 and given the death sentence and he
was replaced by Beria, Stalin's most trusted lieutenant.

When Beria was convicted, Marshal Ivan Konev presided
over the military tribunal side by side with Khrushchev's
appointed prosecutor Roman Rudenko.

Some years ago, a Moscow military court confirmed that
the old verdict reached in December 1953 against Beria and his
group was still "valid" and that everything said and done was in
perfect order. But the question arising is this: Does the Russian

military have the legal standing to impose such a decision on the whole Russian Federation?

It is impossible to know why this pervasive blinkered view of the past is still maintained. Perhaps different groups have different reasons. But one thing is certain: One day the truth will come to light. And there are a couple of hopeful signs indicating that Beria will be seen in a new light these days in contemporary Russia.

Some books on Beria have now been published in Russian, among them the works of Sergei Kremlev, but it is hard to get hold of them. I tried to order three books on Beria at Kubon & Sagner publishing house, among them Beria's diary and two books by Kremlev, but was told that only libraries are supplied with these books. Beria's diary has only been published in Russia. *Russia Today* noted that some excerpts in English language were made public in April 2011, but also Arsen Martinosyan's comment, saying that this diary "surely" was a "forgery."

Another glimmer of hope: according to Prof. Stephan Merl of Bielefeld University, "a Moscow court had to deal with a claim to rehabilitate Beria. In June 2000 it passed a real judgement of Solomon stating that the trial instigated by the July Plenum was based on false accusations. Thus the death sentence had no legal basis. But at the same time the request to rehabilitate him was rejected as Beria under Stalin had no doubt been responsible for killings."[1] Unfortunately, the anti-Beria paradigm is operating even here.

The two verdicts reached by the two Moscow courts clearly show that a fierce battle is now raging over the Beria file.

But one thing is certain: Beria, Stalin's closest colleague, the man who ended Nikolai Yezhov's terror regime and then released more than one hundred thousand prisoners from labor camps and rehabilitated them, who foiled the coup attempt of the Soviet Trotskyites in November 1938 at the last moment — thus saving the Soviet regime from collapse, who organized the resistance against the Nazi aggression during the war years, who also organized the evacuation of Soviet enterprises based in the western part of the USSR to the East, who was instru-

---

[1] in an article formerly cached at: http://www.1000dokumente.de/index.html/
index.html?c=dokument_ru

mental in creating the Soviet A-bomb in the post-war years and who released more than one million inmates from labor camps in 1953, will remain the bogeyman of anti-communist historians, politicians and their associated media for quite a long time.

PART ONE: THE FACTS

The Arrest (Or Murder?) of Beria

On June 26, 1953, something of key importance occurred in Moscow at the highest political level which was going to become a watershed for Soviet socialism: Lavrenti Pavlovich Beria, Soviet Minister of the Interior and the number two in the official Soviet hierarchy after Minister President Malenkov, was violently removed from office and from political life by a group of Soviet officers. Different versions of the event exist and important documents that could provide a clearer picture are still classified after more than 60 years. Let's deal with what Beria's own son, Sergo Beria, had to say about his father's fate and then go over to what other witnesses had to say.

a. Sergo Beria's testimony

Beria's only son, Sergo, was part of the team working on the Soviet hydrogen bomb. He allegedly saw his father on the fateful day. He writes in his book that he was busy in the Kremlin when, all of a sudden, he received a phone call from one of his friends telling him that a terrorist attack had been made on his father's house and that he had seen someone being carried out of the building on a stretcher. Sergo suspects that this man was his own father. He also tells us that his father was not present at the session of the Presidium of the Central Committee of the Communist Party of the Soviet Union during which his father was allegedly arrested by Marshal Zhukov. At this point in time he would no longer have been alive. Some people, he writes, had been afraid that his father could have won the upper hand at this meeting, had he been present. Here the excerpt from his book:

Arrest, Death, Exile.

26 June

We spent that last day with him at the dacha. On 26 June we went for our morning walk together. He had a preoccupied air and told me that he expected difficulties in connection with the Ignatiev affair, which was due to be discussed at the end of the morning.

I went back to the city at 8 a.m. At 10, my colleagues and I were preparing a report on the hydrogen bomb which we were to submit to my father, Malenkov and Bulganin at 4 p.m. My father arrived in Moscow at 9 a.m. His meeting which had been fixed for 12 noon was canceled on the pretext that Ignatiev had fallen ill and had been taken to hospital.

As a rule we lunched together, but as I was at Vannikov's with the papers and the session was to begin at 4 p.m., I stayed there. My father came home to lunch at 12.30.

At about 1 p.m. an airman friend, a Tatar named Amitkhad, telephoned me. He shouted: 'Your father's dead, your house is surrounded. I have a plane ready, I'm coming to look for you and we'll take you to somewhere safe.' I did not believe my ears. It was unthinkable. I tried to telephone, first to our home, then to my office. The lines had been cut and I realized that something was wrong. I spoke to Vannikov, Kurchatov and others, six people in all. It was as though a thunderbolt had fallen on them. They all, like me, took to the telephone. Meanwhile the car came for me...

Having decided to stay, I went back to the office. Kurchatov threw himself upon me. 'Be confident,' he said, 'we'll do everything we can to save your life.'

They tried to contact Malenkov, without success, and then Khrushchev, who replied: 'Don't worry. I'm going to send a car to take him to his mother's. Don't get ideas.' Some men did indeed come for me. I don't know why they took me first to our house. I saw that the windows of my father's bedroom were riddled with bullets. Then doors had been forced. One of our bodyguards who was still there called out to me: 'Sergo! Someone was carried out on a stretcher.' That could only have been my father! Subsequently I spoke with all our servants. They confirmed that everything had happened at our place and not during the meeting of the Presidium.

That same day, tanks had been sent to Moscow. They had taken up positions around the capital at 8 a.m. The Vice-Minister of Internal Affairs, General Maslennikov, telephoned to Shtemenko and Vasilievsky, who did not know what was going on. Nobody could make sense of the situation. Eventually they learned that the order had come from Bulganin. And it was my father who was accused of having attempted a coup d'état!

My father's arrest

There are at least six different versions of the arrest and death of my father. Khrushchev himself provided several variants.

In one of them the principal role is played by Zhukov. The effect is all the better. Hero of the Soviet Union arresting Beria! Many years later Zhukov, to my great surprise, asked to see me. 'I have no reason to lie to you,' he said. 'I took no part, direct or indirect, in the arrest of your father. If he had been alive I would have been at his side. I want you to know that. Do you think that, otherwise, I should have gone with those shits? He added that if my father had still been alive at the time of the July

Plenum, most of the delegates would have sided with him. Mikoyan confirmed that.[1]

b. Skorokhodov's report from *Literaturnaya gazeta,* 27 June, 1988

According to A. Skorokhodov, a military power struggle had taken place between units of the Red Army and troops of the Interior Ministry commanded by Beria (MVD troops). One week before the meeting in the Kremlin, military exercises were organized that he himself had taken part in. Skorokhodov writes that troops of the Moscow air defense, supported by tanks, had been ordered to take up positions near Moscow. The order had been issued by none other than Nikita Khrushchev who, at that time, was just an ordinary secretary of the Central Committee of the CPSU. Officers of the MVD had confronted them and had tried to resist the unit's entry into the city. After 25 years of imposed silence, Skorokhodov wrote:

> I commanded the convoy myself...A sergeant opened the gate wide. The convoy started to move, but soon came to a halt again. On the country road a T 34 tank passed us going at high speed in the direction of Moscow, blackening the road with its exhaust fumes. We noticed that the protective covers had been removed from the cannon and the machine gun. The tank commander was standing in the turret hatch wearing his black uniform and a hood. This command vehicle was followed by a long convoy of tanks...All of a sudden two men in uniform appeared out of the blue, 200 meters in front of the command vehicle: a colonel and a lieutenant of the Interior Ministry with a sub-machine gun as could be judged from his pink epaulets. The short and stocky colonel with a red face blocked the way, raising his arms: "Go back to your barracks at once! I've been authorized by the government to tell all units that all orders have been canceled."

He did not seem to be moving. "I've been given an order by my commander and I'm going to carry it out unless he himself annuls it," I shouted back at him. "You take responsibility for your crime," the colonel shouted furi-

[1] Sergo Beria, *Beria. My Father. Inside Stalin's Kremlin,* London, 2001, pp. 268ff.

ously. "I'm warning you...return to the barracks!" "Don't stand in the way, Colonel! I'm following an order or I'm going to remove you by force."

I told the driver to move on and the colonel jumped to the roadside, helplessly threatening with his fist. Soon the battery reached combat position and combat alarm was given...We had taken up combat position near Moscow. For three days we remained in combat readiness...Only on July 2, we learned that Beria had been the reason for the alarm.

I'm now asking myself why Khrushchev had given orders to the city air-defense to adopt combat readiness...Only gradually it dawned on me that this had been absolutely necessary. One had to take into account that Beria still had many sincere followers among the MVD troops, and in state security as well, who not just dutifully but completely convincingly defended a well-functioning retaliation system. What would have happened if the principled and resolute General Moskalenko had not succeeded in bringing his military police into the Kremlin before Beria's loyal units had arrived there?"[1]

Skorokhodov's belated report suggests that the liquidation of Beria in late June of 1953 was planned with military precision and that Khrushchev, in his capacity of party secretary, but not as party leader, gave orders to mobilize the Soviet army and the Moscow air defense forces to take action against the forces of the Interior Ministry; and that his co-conspirator, Marshal Moskalenko, the commander of the Moscow air defense forces, even sent military police to the Kremlin, apparently to make sure that Beria and his allies had no chance to foil the coup. If we can believe this report, a full-blown coup d'état had taken place, most probably organized by Nikita Khrushchev and high-ranking military officers.

c. Khrushchev's contradictory versions of the events

Khrushchev during his period in office spread different versions of what went on in the Kremlin in late June of 1953.

---

[1] A. Skorokhodov, *How we were Prepared for the Battle with Beria*, in: Vladimir F. Nekrassow, *Berija — Henker in Stalins Diensten*, Augsburg 1997, pp. 353ff.

Once he told Italian communists that Beria was shot at the session of the Presidium (Politburo) on June 26 by military men; on another occasion he boasted that he himself had fired a shot at Beria; and once he even claimed that Beria was strangled by some members at this meeting. When meeting the French socialist senator Pierre Commin in Moscow in 1956, he told him this:

> Soon after Stalin's death we received reports in the Presidium [the renamed former Politburo, the highest party body — author] on some double game Beria was playing. We had him observed and after a couple of weeks realized that our suspicion was justified. He was obviously planning a conspiracy against the Presidium. Having been waiting for a favorable moment, we convened a session of the Presidium to which, of course, also Beria was invited. He turned up, being apparently totally unaware of what we all knew. We then interrogated him, stated and quoted facts, asked him questions — in other words: we cross-examined him for four hours.
>
> We all knew that he was guilty and that this man could be dangerous for both the Party and the country.
>
> We left him alone in the room, here in this room where we are now talking to each other, and he sat on the seat you're now sitting on. Then we went into another room to discuss what we should do with him. We were absolutely convinced of his guilt, but at that time we didn't have enough conclusive evidence to take him to court, but it was impossible to release him. We then decided unanimously to shoot him on the spot as this was the only option to prevent a revolution. This decision was carried out immediately. When we received sufficient and irrefutable evidence of his guilt some time after his condemnation we felt much better.[1]

Khrushchev does not tell us who shot and killed Beria "on the spot." In his memoirs he never mentioned this variant again. There he spread this version of the June events:

---

[1] Georg Paloczi-Horwarth, *Chruschtschow*, Frankfurt/Main 1961, pp. 147f, citing Bertrand Wolfe.

After everybody had made his statement, Malenkov as chairman was asked to sum up the main points and to formulate a common declaration, but at the last moment he started panicking and after the last speech the meeting was interrupted. A long pause ensued. I realized that we were in a tight spot. Then I asked Comrade Malenkov to be given the floor to propose a motion. As we had agreed in advance, I proposed that the Presidium should release Beria from his duties as Deputy Chairman of the Council of Ministers and as Minister for Internal Affairs and to also remove him from all government posts that he occupied. Malenkov was still being panicky. As far as I can remember, he didn't even put my motion to a vote. He then pressed a secret button giving a signal to the generals waiting in the adjacent room. Zhukov came in first, followed by Moskalenko and the others. Then Malenkov said to Comrade Zhukov: "As chairman of the Council of Ministers I ask you to take Beria into custody pending an examination of all the accusations raised against him!"

"Hands up!" Zhukov told Beria...

Beria was soon brought to the building of the Council of Ministers, kept in a room next to Malenkov's office and put under guard. Now a new question camp up: Where could we take Beria after having detained him?...We finally agreed to hand him over to Comrade Moskalenko, the commander of the air defense forces who then ordered his people to take Beria to a bunker near his headquarters. I made sure that General Moskalenko did everything possible which was necessary to serve the interests of the Party...When Rudenko began with the interrogations, we realized that we were dealing with a really terrible man, with a beast to whom nothing was sacred. When we opened the archives and put him on trial, we saw what kind of methods Beria had used to reach his goals. Not only did he have anything communist in him but also not the slightest traits of human decency.[1]

---

[1] Strobe Talbott, ed., *Chruschtschow erinnert sich. Die authentischen Memoiren*, Reinbek/Hamburg 1992, pp. 314ff.

According to this version, Beria was not "shot on the spot," as Khrushchev told us previously, but taken into custody, questioned by chief prosecutor Roman Rudenko (appointed by Khrushchev after Stalin's death -author) to await his trial in December the same year.

When Zhukov was deposed as Defense Minister by Khrushchev in October 1957 while visiting Yugoslavia and Albania, Khrushchev ceased to mention his name in connection with Beria's arrest.

How to explain the different versions presented by Khrushchev on the events? Why did he choose on one occasion the one and on another a different story? Khrushchev's son-in-law Alexey Adshubei, who knew his father-in-law well, said that in July 1953, when Beria had been removed, he thought that his hour had finally come and from now on he told the story all over again, even to his bodyguards, giving new details and embellishing one or the other part of it. He says that this event had been his proudest moment:

> During the November 1960 world conference of Communist Parties, an emotional Khrushchev shocked Soviet and foreign guests by describing how Malenkov "went white" at the climatic moment and had to be "kicked under the table" and how Beria "was all green and shit in his pants." What made Khrushchev's victory all the sweeter, according to Konstantin Simonov, was that Beria considered him "a fat, clumsy, red-mugged fool whom he, Beria, ... could wrap around his finger."[1]

d. Molotov's story

V. Molotov, the long-time Soviet Foreign Minister, who was present at the Presidium meeting on June 26, 1953, when Beria was arrested, made the following statements in various interviews he gave his biography Felix Chuev in the seventies and eighties:

> He was arrested during the Politburo session (Molotov calls the Presidium still "Politburo" - author). Discussion ensued. Malenkov chaired. I don't remember who first

---

[1] William Taubman, *Khrushchev. The Man and his Era*, New York and London, 2003, p. 258.

took the floor. I was among the first to speak, possibly even the first or second speaker. The session began in the usual manner. We were all friends. Since we had agreed beforehand to have Beria arrested during the session, it was initially made to look like a normal session, but later it changed...Someone apparently suggested that Beria's conduct had to be discussed, and I was one of the first to speak. I said that Beria was a degenerate, that he could not be taken seriously, and that he was no communist. Perhaps he was a communist at some time in the past, but he was a degenerate now, and alien to the party. That was the essence of my remarks. I did not know Beria's past well. I had just heard some rumors and all kinds of talk...

Then Beria took the floor to defend himself. No one was prevented from speaking. He said, "Of course I have made mistakes, but I ask you not to expel me from the party. I've always carried out the party's decisions and Stalin's directives. Stalin entrusted me with the most critical and secret matters. And I have always duly completed them. So it would be wrong to expel me..."

No, he was no fool. Malenkov pressed the button...Beria had arrived at the session totally unaware of what lay in store for him...

The room was securely guarded, but sitting in Proskreby-shev's room (A. N. Proskrebyshev was Stalin's personal secretary and member of the Central Committee who was arrested shortly before Stalin died in early March 1953-author), which adjoined the meeting room, was a group of military officers headed by Zhukov. The group was waiting to be called in to arrest Beria. Malenkov pressed the button. That was the signal. Malenkov chaired the session, so he controlled the button. The group of officers led by Zhukov entered the room.

Malenkov: "Arrest Beria!"...

Malenkov's performance precisely showed the good side of his character...Khrushchev appeared to have started this plan with me. And I said that I consented. I have no regrets about it now. On the contrary, I believed and I continue to believe, that this was to Khrushchev's great credit. That's my opinion...

"I fell into a trap!" he (Beria — author) cried. He didn't expect that from Khrushchev.

Moskalenko also was involved. Khrushchev had him promoted to marshal...Moskalenko was put in charge of the jail where Beria was kept. That seems to be the reason for the promotion, which was definitely initiated by Khrushchev.[1]

In Molotov's account there also is no talk about Beria having been killed on the spot or fired at by a heroic Khrushchev. Beria obviously was the victim of a set-up, was lured to the Presidium meeting, was totally unaware of what was going to happen to him, fell in a trap, was arrested during the meeting by a group of high-ranking Soviet officers, among them Georgi Zhukov, and kept in jail to await his trial at the end of the year that condemned him to death and had him executed immediately after trial together with six of his collaborators. Maybe his house has also been raided by a special unit to arrest him there prior to the session, as his son Sergo wants to tell us. Khrushchev seems to have been the chief organizer of it all, but Molotov was also involved as he admitted himself.

e. Zhukov's account

Malenkov told us how the operation was going to be carried out: The meeting of the Council of Ministers is canceled, instead a session of the Presidium is convened. I was told to wait in a room adjoining the meeting room together with Moskalenko, Nedelin, Batitsky, and Moskalenko's aide until a bell would ring twice. I was warned: Beria was said to be strong and a judoka. "We shall get it done, we're no weaklings."

So we were waiting in the side room, and had been waiting for an hour already. Had anything happened inside without our knowledge? Had Beria, this intriguer and Stalin confidant, managed to outwit the others?

---

[1] Albert Resis, ed., *Molotov Remembers. Inside Kremlin Politics*, Conversations with Felix Chuev, Chicago, 1993, pp. 344ff.

Around one o'clock the bell rang, first once then twice. I stood up first...We entered the room. Beria sat at the table in the middle. My generals walked around the table as if they intended to sit at the wall. I positioned myself behind Beria and said: "Stand up, you're under arrest!"

Before he was able to stand up, I tore his arms backwards and pushed him up. He was pale and did not move. We led him through the anteroom and took him to another room with an emergency exit. There we searched him.

Oh yes, there is still another thing: When I grabbed Beria, I checked at once to make sure he wasn't carrying a weapon. Only one of us had a pistol. We then managed to get hold of another one. We had no idea why we were called into the Kremlin, so we were without any weapons. Beria, too, didn't have a weapon. When he stood up, I gave his briefcase which was filled with documents a push so that it slid over the long polished table.

In the room I mentioned we guarded him until 10 p.m. Then we took him out of the Kremlin. We pushed him onto the back seat of a ZIZ car and covered him with a carpet. The Kremlin guards, who were subordinate to him as Minister of the Interior, was not suspicious and let us pass. Moskalenko was driving. Beria was brought to the main police station, or to be more precise, to the prison of the Moscow military district. There he remained all the time during the investigations and during the trial. And there he was also executed.[1]

So, Beria was not "shot on the spot" as Khrushchev once claimed but was arrested and brought to a military jail for interrogation. The kidnapped Minister of the Interior was smuggled out of the Kremlin in a government car so as not to arise any suspicion like in a James Bond movie. Zhukov, who later told Beria's son that he didn't have anything to do with his father's arrest, here proudly admits to have arrested Beria and to have been briefed by Malenkov beforehand about what was going to happen. His statement that he had no idea why his group was

---

[1] Vladimir F. Nekrassow, ed., *Berija — Henker in Stalins Diensten*, ibid., pp. 343f.

called into the Kremlin and that he had no weapon upon him seems highly unlikely.

f. Other testimonies

Air-force General Kyrill Moskalenko, Zhukov's and Khrushchev's co-conspirator, also wrote a report on Beria's arrest which is likewise included in Nekrassov's book.

There he says that he had been informed about the forthcoming arrest one day in advance by Khrushchev and was told to bring weapons with him. Moskalenko also mentions future Soviet leader Leonid Brezhnev's participation in the coup and that Prime Minister Malenkov was heavily involved. According to his statement, Zhukov, however, had not been involved in the kidnapping, but had returned home before all that happened. He said that Marshal Bulganin — later to become Khrushchev's Prime Minister — had proposed to decorate all officers who took part in the operation with the medal "Hero of the Soviet Union," something he himself had however rejected. Moskalenko also claims that he took part in Beria's interrogation lasting a full six months, starting in July. Beria had not been executed before the December trial, he said.

But this is challenged by what Stalin's daughter, Svetlana Alliluyeva, tells us. She said that Beria was executed shortly after his arrest and did not take part in the trial. Maybe she had it from hearsay.

This is contradicted by a Soviet officer by the name of Zergatskov who claimed to have been present at the trial as a military observer. He later told Albanian Communist leader, Enver Hoxha, that he had witnessed how forcefully and courageously Beria had defended himself during trial. And there is another witness: Member of the military tribunal Kuchava, who was also present in his capacity of a Georgian trade unionist. In an interview he gave years later the maintained that he had seen Beria in the court room.

In early July (1953), a few days after his arrest, Beria wrote a letter to his former comrade Malenkov which can be read in the appendix. This proves (if the letter is genuine) that Beria was not shot or "strangled" (Khrushchev) at the Presidium session and was also not assassinated in his house as his son Sergo claimed in his book on his father.

Minutes of the Presidium session of June 26 do not exist, or they are still classified and kept in a remote place in the archives of the Russian Federation. But a shorthand record of the Plenum of the Central Committee that took place a week later does exist. It was convened from July 2–7. This document was kept in the archives of the Soviet Union for almost forty years and was finally declassified in 1991 when the Soviet Union was about to collapse. Originally, this record was only made available to the participants of the aforementioned plenum.

Three days after Beria's arrest, another Presidium meeting is convened, most probably to prepare the forthcoming plenum in great detail. At the plenum itself Beria's and Stalin's long-time collaborators, among them Molotov, Malenkov, Voroshilov, and Kaganovich, who in the summer of 1957 tried to depose Khrushchev but failed, approved of the operation wholeheart-edly and let his former comrade down to side with Khrushchev and his other conspirators. Molotov defended the operation in his memoirs, using similar phrases he had been using after the events. But shortly before his death in 1986, he seemed to have changed his attitude towards Beria and called him someone who had been absolutely loyal to the Soviet Union.

So what do we know?

Lavrenti Pavlovich Beria, the Soviet Secretary (or Minister) of the Interior and head of the Soviet security apparatus after Stalin's sudden death on March 5, 1953, who had launched a whole series of reform initiatives to overhaul the Soviet political system after Stalin's death, was detained by a group of high-ranking Soviet marshals and other officers and not just put under house arrest, but kept in military confinement. Nikita Khrush-chev, the chief organizer of his arrest, was working hand in glove with this group and got the support of the rest of the Soviet Presidium, among them Molotov and Malenkov, in carrying out the operation. How exactly his arrest, which must be called a blatant kidnapping, took place and what was going on prior to it at the crucial Presidium meeting which was convened at short notice, we don't really know as there are different and sometimes contradictory accounts and no official record exists or it exists but is still kept classified in the archives. It seems certain that he was not shot "on the spot" or "strangled" as Khrushchev once claimed but immediately brought out of the Kremlin in a government car, put in a military prison and then handed over to air-force marshal Moskalenko and the new Soviet prosecutor Roman Rudenko, who interrogated him pending his trial in December. Reports of court proceedings as to this trial do also not exist. Beria and a group of his collaborators were shot immediately after trial and their belongings confiscated. He was given no defense counsel and had no right of appeal. Neither a grave nor a gravestone exists of Beria, and up to the present day he is defamed and called a "monster" by some, a sexual predator or sadist by others.

Only the opening of the archives could shed more light on what exactly happened in late June/early July of 1953 or during his trial in December. What he did and what he achieved during his lifetime as a Bolshevik, especially in his home country Georgia, where he once was leader of the Georgian Communist Party, is almost never mentioned. The official Russian media still slander and libel him and stick to the version widely spread by his adversaries.

Those generals who took part in Beria's arrest were later rewarded for their "services": Zhukov was later appointed Soviet Defense Minister; Moskalenko was promoted to the rank of Marshal of the Soviet Union by Khrushchev and Leonid Brezhnev, who also belonged to the group of officers involved in the capture of Beria, became one of Khrushchev's permanent protégés.

A word about Beria's collaborators who were also arrested, put on trial and executed, among them Vladimir G. Dekanozov, once Stalin's ambassador to Berlin: These people were later arrested by Khrushchev's secret service men, Ivan A. Serov and Sergey N. Kruglov. Beria's son Sergo was also arrested, as was Beria's wife Nino. Sergo Beria was kept in prison for years.

Between 1954 and 1956 more (political) arrests and so-called "trials" were organized by Khrushchev's supporters to liquidate those politicians who had been loyal to Stalin and Beria, among them Viktor Abakumov, former head of the Soviet MGB, arrested already in 1951. The last in a long series to be arrested and executed for political reasons in the mid-fifties was the Azerbaijani party leader Bagirov, who supported Stalin. He was put on trial in 1956.

The Plenum of the Central Committee of the Communist Party of the Soviet Union, July 2–7, 1953

One week after the violent removal of Beria from the political scene, a plenum of the Central Committee of the CPSU took place in the Kremlin. The only item on the agenda: Beria's case.

Although it had been a long-standing tradition since the time of Lenin that the Chairman of the Council of Ministers also chaired the plenum sessions, Georgi Malenkov, the chairman of the Council of Ministers of the USSR, was not allowed to preside over the meeting but rather the rising star Nikita Khrushchev who, at that time, officially speaking, was nothing but the Secretary of the Central Committee. Clearly, Khrushchev had benefited most from Beria's ousting and had become the number one in the political hierarchy, also because he enjoyed the full support of top army officers like Marshals Georgi Zhukov and Kyrill Moskalenko.

The speeches made by the ordinary members of the Central Committee, who did not belong to the Presidium, broadly followed the line predetermined by the top politicians of the Presidium. Malenkov, Khrushchev, Kaganovich, Molotov, Bulganin made the first speeches, which were then followed by similar speeches using similar phrases and terminology. No single ordinary member of the Central Committee dared to dissent from the prescribed line by the chief party bosses; nobody dared to defend Beria and his supporters in the Soviet Security Services, with the sole exception of the Azerbaijani party leader Bagirov, who at one point of Khrushchev's speech, interrupted him, shouting that no evidence existed of Beria's alleged spying activities in the twenties for foreign intelligence services as claimed by Khrushchev & Co. Even former followers of Beria, among them the CC members Bakradze and Mirzchulava, joined in the abuse of Beria, apparently in an effort to save their own skin (see Viktor Knoll und Lothar Kölm, *Der Fall Berija — Protokoll einer Abrechnung*, Berlin, 1999).

On July 7, the last day of the session, a resolution was passed comprising seven points, entitled: *On the Criminal Activities of Beria Against the Party and the State*. It was adopted unanimously with no abstentions. On this last day of the four-day-long plenum, Khrushchev rewarded the man who obviously played the key role to make the operation a success: Soviet Marshal Georgi Zhukov. He proposed to grant him the status of a candidate of the Central Committee. Another of Khrushchev's followers, former chief of the Soviet State Security, S. D. Ignatiev, who had been expelled from the party on June 2 for deceitful and dishonest behavior, was not only given back his membership card but was also reelected member of the Central Committee at Khrushchev's request. In 1952, Ignatiev withheld a memorandum on the question whether the US army was using biological weapons in the Korean War and tried to keep it secret.[1] So Khrushchev just ignored a decision of the party's Control Commission in an effort to rehabilitate one of his cronies in a clear breach of party rules.

On the other hand: Two of Beria's confidants who should later also be charged with treason and included in the December trial, Golidze and Kobulov, are stripped of their status of candidates to the Central Committee at Khrushchev's request. The reason given by Khrushchev: Their allegedly "hostile activities against the party and the Soviet state." This way he skillfully used Beria's condemnation to purge the CC of other Beria supporters.

Malenkov, still chairman of the Soviet Council of Ministers, made the closing speech. From the outside it looked as if the party was now more united and stronger than ever.

Beria himself, who was once awarded the Order of Lenin for having supervised the construction of the Soviet A-bomb, could not defend himself any more at the meeting. He was now being abused by the delegates, using some of the following derogatory

---

[1] http://digitalarchive.wilsoncenter.org/document/113754

words and phrases:[1] provocateur, rogue, agent, spy of foreign secret services, among them the British, deceiver, degenerate, filthy, devious traitor, enemy of the people, enemy of the party, arch-enemy, enemy of the state, unscrupulous like a Judas, careerist, crafty, criminal, hypocrite, despicable, bourgeois nationalist, egoist, snake, sadist, blind, evil bureaucrat, arrogant, tactless, pest, dangerous adventurer, conspirator, monster, cancer, intriguer, self-admirer, malicious agitator, scoundrel, vulgar, filthy, counterrevolutionary, fascist, slanderer, refuse, beast, agent of the class enemy, defeatist, rapist, bourgeois surrogate, deformed person, potato thief, unbridled, womanizer, saboteur, cunning, false, insidious, dictator, a man who hasn't read a single book (Molotov), nauseating, synonym for craftiness, insidiousness and breach of trust, etc., etc.

It is striking that Khrushchev used similar terms during his time in the Ukraine as party chief in 1938, when he was member of a troika (a court consisting of three people) to catch "enemies of the people" and "traitors," posing as a staunch Stalinist. More than 50,000 people were arrested and thousands of them executed under false charges, and it was Beria, called in by Stalin from Georgia, who then put an end to the madness arresting Nikolai Yezhov, the former head of the Soviet Secret Service, Minister of the Interior and instigator of the witch-hunts.

Beria then released more than one hundred thousand people from labor camps and prisons. Grover Furr wrote:

> Many — certainly more than 100,000 — persons wrongly repressed were released from GULAG camps and prisons.[2]

It is also quite significant how many speakers not belonging to the Presidium do their utmost to curry favor with Khrushchev, the new strong man, and with the other members of the highest party body. Many refer to their previous speeches repeating the words and phrases used by them. Some heap praise on the new party leader and his "vigilance."

---

[1] The selection is from Viktor Knoll and Lothar Kölm, *Der Fall Berija. Protokoll einer Abrechnung*, Berlin, 1999)

[2] Grover Furr, *Khrushchev Lied*, ibid., p. 75, quoting Okhotin and Roginsky in Danilov, V., et al, *Tragedia Soetskoi Derevni*, vol. 5, No. 2 (Moscow: ROSSPEN 2006), p. 517.

One of those who broke all the records set by the previous orators was Lazar Kaganovich, under whose guidance Khrushchev started his career as an "expert" on agricultural matters. He called Beria a "fascist" who had supposedly planned a "fascist putsch." But V. Molotov, who had worked side by side with Beria for years on end, especially during the Great Patriotic War, did not pull his punches either. Molotov disqualifies Beria this way: He is a "traitor and enemy of our party and Soviet state"; "Beria has been exposed"; he showed "criminal behavior"; "a dirty and amoral type"; "a great criminal"; "a narrow-minded person"; "he had a plan against the construction of Communism in our country and kept it secret"; he was an "agent of the class enemy" and an "agent of imperialism"; he was involved in "shady dealings and swindling"; he used "methods hostile to the party"; he "played a villainous role," and the list goes on. In his memoirs Molotov repeats many of the accusations, adding even some new ones like "Beria — parasite on the party," without providing any evidence whatsoever.

Only four years later, Molotov himself was called "an enemy of the party" when he tried to depose Khrushchev, together with some of his allies in the Presidium, among them Kaganovich, Malenkov and Voroshilov. He was then expelled from the party and the group was said to have been an "Anti-Party-Group." But here, he is a loyal ally of Khrushchev and runs with the pack. The same holds true for Malenkov and Kaganovich, once loyal collaborators of Stalin who knew Beria from times of war where they met in regular intervals to organize the resistance against the Nazi coalition that had invaded the country in the summer of 1941. Their speeches were later used as munition to prepare Beria's trial and subsequent execution.

Khrushchev in his speech at the Plenum still pretended to be an ally of the deceased Stalin:

> This is a devious person and a skilled careerist. With his dirty paws he held Stalin's soul tightly in his hands, and he knew well how to impose his opinion on him.[1]

---

[1] Viktor Knoll and Lothar Kölm, eds., *Der Fall Berija — Protokoll einer Abrechnung*, Berlin, 1999, p. 47.

Years later, when he went into the offensive to denounce and slander Stalin as well, he said that Beria was Stalin's product. Stalin had his henchmen and Beria had been one of them to "kill honest people with his help," etc. But at this point in time — Stalin was still in high esteem in the party and the country, and only four months had passed since his death in March — he could not slander him without risking a storm of protest. But it was a different story with Beria, who had never enjoyed Stalin's high reputation and who now had been arrested by the "hero of the Soviet Union," Marshal of the Soviet Union Georgi K. Zhukov. This man had liberated Berlin in 1945, and the feared Beria was now out of the way and spending his time in a military bunker (if he was still alive, that is). When he was still around, Khrushchev never dared to say a bad word about him and tried to win his "friendship."

But it was Khrushchev's close ally Nikolai N. Shatalin who surpassed all the other slanderers when making the following statement, quoting Beria's bodyguard Sarkissov, who suppos-edly had slipped Shatalin this piece of information:

> Beria told me to keep a separate list of women with whom he had sexual intercourse (laughter in the hall). Later I was told by him to destroy the list. But one of these lists I kept to myself nevertheless. This list contains names, first names, addresses, and telephone numbers of more than 25 of such women. I still have the list at home in the pocket of my military jacket...A year or a year and a half ago, I found out without doubt that Beria suffered from syphilis due to his relations with prostitutes...

> This, comrades, is Beria's true face, this applicant for the title of the leader of the Soviet people. And this stray dog has dared to challenge a giant like our party and the Central Committee.[1]

According to the minutes, Shatalin's speech met with approval.

Beria's wife Nino, who was also arrested after the June events in the Kremlin, later said in an interview that these allegations were totally untrue. Her husband never had such relations and

---

[1] Ibid., p. 233.

was working all day. During his trial half a year later, all these allegations and "findings" were again used to make Beria appear to have been a moral degenerate and to justify the death sentence. At the plenum, Shatalin's "findings" were highly welcome since this story could serve the purpose to unite the entire party body behind Khrushchev and the other party bosses, and even Beria's former Georgian coworkers then voted for the anti-Beria resolution on the last day of the meeting.

The Secret Trial Against Beria, Merkulov, Dekanozov and Others, Dec. 18-23, 1953

No documents and other materials referring to the secret trial of the military tribunal against Beria and his Georgian collaborators in the security services of the Soviet Union have been released by the Russian Federation, as has already been mentioned. In Vladimir Nekrassov's book on Beria (*Beria — Hangman in Stalin's Services*, German title: *Berija — Henker in Stalins Diensten*, August, 1997) authors like B. Popov and V. Opperkov are quoted, who apparently belonged to those trusted historians who were given exceptional access to the archives. But their statements only refer to the composition of the trial jury, to the names of the accused and to the wording of the indictment. The two authors published a series of articles entitled *The Era of Beria* in *Woino istoricheski shurnal* (*Military Historical Journal*) in 1989 and 1990, during the Era of Gorbachev's Perestroika.

If we can believe the two authors, the following persons took part in the military trial:

> From December 18-23, 1953, the trial of the Special Court of the Supreme Court of the USSR took place in Moscow which was closed to the public. Chairman of the court was Marshal of the Soviet Union, I. S. Konev, as was noted in the report. Other members were: N. V. Shvernik, Chairman of the Central Council of the Trade Unions of the Soviet Union; Y. L. Zeidin, First Deputy of the Chairman of the Supreme Court of the Soviet Union; Army General K. S. Moskalenko; N. A. Michailov, First Secretary of the Moscow District Committee of the CPSU; M. A. Kuchava, Chairman of the Georgian

Council of Trade Unions; L. A. Gromov, Chairman of the Moscow City Court; K. F. Lunev, First Deputy of the Minister of the Interior of the USSR.[1]

This would mean the following:

1. A person who was directly involved in Beria's arrest like air-force General Kyrill Moskalenko was also a member of the military tribunal, acting as a judge — a clear breach of internationally recognized legal principles.

2. The Chairman of the special judicial panel was a high-ranking army officer who had no legal background and no qualifications as a judge either. Marshal Konev only represented the interests of parts of the Soviet military that was highly involved in Beria's kidnapping. Again: judge and prosecutor in one person.

3. Beria and the other accused had not been given a defense lawyer; they had to defend themselves.

4. The trial was closed to the general public.

5. No appeal against the sentence was possible. The verdict was executed on the spot, i.e., the persons who had acted as high Soviet officials for years under Stalin, among them Beria and Dekanozov, were found guilty of treason and shot immediately after trial, and their property was confiscated.

6. Non-military judges were also allowed to preside over the proceedings, among them trade union and party officials, who also do not seem to have any legal or constitutional qualifications.

The trial was prepared by prosecutor Roman Rudenko, a friend of Khrushchev from his time in the Ukraine where he used to be party chief in the late thirties. Rudenko was Khrushchev's chief prosecutor in Ukraine at the time and helped Khrushchev there to purge the Ukrainian Communist Party and the Ukrainian state thoroughly from "enemies of the people" (i.e., honest communists and many working people) during the time of the "Great Terror," also referred to as the "Yezhovshina" (see William

---

[1] B. Popow/V. Oppokov, *Die Berija-Zeit*, in: Vladimir F. Nekrassow, ibid., p. 369.

Taubman, *Khrushchev. The Man and his Era,* ibid., p. 256). Shortly before Beria's trial, former General Prosecutor Safronov was put out of harm's way, as Khrushchev proudly puts it in his memoirs, because in his opinion he was "not trustworthy".

As the Procurator-General of the Soviet Union was appointed by the Supreme Soviet for seven years according to the constitution of 1936, which at that time was still valid, and Safronov's term had not come to an end, Rudenko was made his successor unconstitutionally.

Rudenko said that he and his deputy had investigated Beria's case "for six months," from late July till December, when the trial started. This suggests that even before Beria's arrest he and his deputy had started collecting incriminating material against him — not just for the trial but also for the crucial Presidium session on June 26.

Soviet Marshal Ivan Konev then is said to have opened the proceedings on December 18 at 10 a.m. using the following words(if we can trust the two above-mentioned authors):

> The session of the Special Panel of the Supreme Court of the USSR is opened. The accused are: BERIA, Lavrenti Pavlovich; MERKULOV, Vsevolod Nikolayevich; DEKANOZOV, Vladmir Georgivich, KOBULOV, Bogdan Sakharyevich; GOLIDZE, Sergei Arsenyevich; MESCHIK, Pavel Yakovlevich; WLODSIMIRSKI, Lev Yemelyanovich...We now proceed to the taking of evidence. Comrade Secretary, please read out the indictment...[1]

Beria was then stripped of all of the titles, ranks and decorations he had received before and during the war, among them the rank of marshal he was given in recognition of his activities during the Great Patriotic War.

What is known about the trial itself? Since we do not possess an official record and in view of the fact that the participating judges did not take any notes for later publication we depend on the testimonies of people who claim to have been given permission to observe the proceedings as a guest.

---

[1] B. Popov/V. Oppokov, *Die Berija-Zeit,* in: Vladimir F. Nekrassow, ibid.

a. The "witness" Alexei Yakushek

In the early sixties, Yakushek, a former philosophy professor, defected to the West and years later, in 1969, wrote a report for the West German news magazine *Der Spiegel* in which he claims to have been present at Beria's trial. The trial, he says, took place in the great hall of the Soviet Trade Union Federation which can house more than a hundred visitors, meaning that, contrary to the official version, a selected part of the general public had been allowed to watch the trial.

He then makes some remarks on the proceedings, that on the day he was present the long list of women Beria was said to have raped, was read out which, as Yakushek claims, had bored Beria. Then more details were made on the type of sex orgies Beria was said to have taken part in.

There are serious doubts as to whether Yakushek's statements are reliable:

First: Yakushek says that the trial started on December 14, although we know for sure that it started later, on December 18.

Second: He claims to have been given a visitors' card by "Khrushchev's adopted son by the name of Vladimir Trush," allegedly one of his examination candidates. Khrushchev, however, did not have an adopted son, just an adopted daughter called Yuliya.

Third: He maintains that the accused had been given lawyers which is not true. Even the official version does not mention any legal counsels whatsoever.

So it seems that Yakushek has made up this story to create the impression that the trial was relatively fair after all and that Beria really was a sexual predator as has been alleged by his adversaries so many times. Maybe he tried to earn some money by inventing this story or he just wanted to get into the public eye (*Der Spiegel*, No. 50/1969, A. Yakushek, *Ich war immer der Partei ergeben — I've always been loyal to the party*).

b. Beria's son Sergo

In his book on his father (*Beria. My Father*, London, 2001) Sergo Beria also mentions what the then deputy procurator-general Tsaregradsky told him shortly after his release from prison:

When I was released, Tsaregradsky came to fetch me from my cell. Once we were outside he said to me: "It was I who wrote the minutes of the interrogation of your father."

"Why didn't you show them to me?"

"There was nothing to show. I wrote them."

"What do you mean?"

"Hundreds of people were interrogated."

So, then it was on the basis of those testimonies that he had composed the minutes...without even seeing my father![1]

He also states that two former judges of the special court, Shvernik and Mikhailov, who had approved of the verdict, told him after his release from prison that they had not seen his father in the courtroom. Mikhailov allegedly said to them this:

Another member of the tribunal, Mikhailov, was the Secretary of the Central Committee of the Komsomol or of the Party organization in Moscow. His son worked at my institute. I invited him to the dacha of my mother-in-law. "Sergo, I don't want to give you details, but we did not see your father alive," he confessed to me. After that meeting with him, his son said to me: "You can believe my father. All the time the trial was on, he was gloomy and silent."[2]

Shvernik, the trade union official, who had also been on the panel of judges, greeted him when he had returned from exile (after his release from prison, he was sent into exile), saying:

He told me with a sad smile: "I was a member of the tribunal, but did not see your father even once."[3]

c. M. Kuchava

Mitrofan Ionovich Kuchava, a Georgian trade union official, also took part in the trial as an ordinary member of the panel of

---

[1] Sergo Beria, *Beria. My Father*, ibid., p. 274.
[2] Ibid., p. 275.
[3] Ibid.

judges. In July 1990, the 84-year-old man and last living member of the panel gave Vladimir Nekrassov, the author of the afore-mentioned book, an interview on the topic, saying that he had recognized Beria in the courtroom and that he had made a final statement on the last day of the proceedings:

> So I can say with certainty that it was Beria who sat in the dock (he had met Beria four times altogether in his lifetime — author). During the six days the trial lasted, Beria gave answers to different and concrete questions a "double" of him could simply not have answered, and who would have been prepared to be shot instead of him?[1]

Kuchava, however, does not refer to what Beria exactly said in court and what he had heard him say (apart from giving a general, very negative impression of him), but only quotes from certain dubious case files and minutes of interrogations (Nekrassov, ibid., pp. 366f). All these "sources" are not made available in Nekrassov's book on Beria, although the author obviously has had access to the archives and could therefore have quoted them in detail. Apart from that, Nekrassov's book is extremely biased against Beria.

Usually, Russian sources are cited this way: First the name of the archive in abbreviated form is mentioned, for example: AVP RF stands for Archive for Foreign Affairs of the Russian Federation, after that "fond" (inventory or stock) is given, then comes "opis" (index), after that "papka"(file) and finally "port" (access). The type of the document is also mentioned, be it a telegram, a resolution, a conversation, an interrogation, etc. If the document has been translated, the name of the translator is added. All these typical characteristics are missing from Kucha-va's report. Nekrassov is trying to give him credibility by making a short introduction where it says that he is the "last still living member of the Special Panel of Judges of the Supreme Court of the USSR," but that is all.

d. Vladimir F. Nekrassov

In his book on Beria Nekrassov also includes an article of his own entitled, *Das Finale der Macht — nach Akten des Gerichtsprozesses*

---

[1] Vladimir F. Nekrassov, ibid., p. 365.

(engl.: Endgame of Power — Court Files). There he claims to have had access to the court files and quotes from Beria's inter-rogation without adding the source. In one of his excerpts from an alleged shorthand text on one of Beria's interrogations by Procurator-General Rudenko we find the following dialogue:

Rudenko: "Do you admit your punishable moral depravity?"

Beria: "Yes, I must admit to be guilty in a way."

R.: "Do you admit that in your punishable moral depravity you went as far as contacting women who were working for foreign intelligence agencies?"

B.: "It's possible. But I don't know."

R.: "At your request, Sarkissov and Nadariya were told to keep a record on your sweethearts. Here I have nine lists with the names of 62 women. Are these the lists of your sweethearts?"

B.: "With most of the women mentioned in the lists I had a relationship."

R.: "Apart from that, Nadariya had 32 lists with addresses of women. Did you also have intimate relations with these women?"

B.: "Yes, they were also my mistresses."

R.: "Did you suffer from syphilis?"

B.: "Yes, during the war. I believe I had syphilis in 1943. I underwent treatment and was cured."[1]

Sarkissov is the name of one of Beria's bodyguards who was mentioned by Nikolai Shatalin in his speech to the delegates of the July plenum of the Central Committee of the CPSU. There the allegations of Beria's "immoral character" were made for the first time, in an apparent attempt to commit character assas-sination. Now these early allegations, or fabrications rather, are again referred to and are made use of to "prove" that Beria was a "pervert" or a "moral degenerate" or both and was rightly

---

[1] Ibid., p. 461.

arrested and condemned to death, independent of all the other accusations of a more political nature.

As if the already said was not enough, Nekrassov then adds the following story:

> Beria was accused to have raped a schoolgirl of the 7th grade who then had a son from him. Beria however declared that he did not use violence against her.[1]

All this raises the following questions:

First: If Beria had all this admitted in the course of his interrogations, why didn't they let him admit it and prove his "moral depravity" publicly in an open trial, to show to the world that he really was such a "despicable degenerate"? This would have been much more convincing and effective than keeping everything top secret. Why did the trial take place behind closed doors at all? The only reason for a closed trial could have been military secrets; but no military issues were at stake and had to be discussed at the trial.

Second: Kuchava,, who says that he recognized Beria in the courtroom does not tell us anything about Beria confessing anything of that nature during the trial; instead he refers to some highly doubtful material from his interrogations. If Beria had actually been present at the trial, he would have been questioned on these issues in Kuchava's presence and he could have referred to his answers, which he does not.

Third: The monstrosity of the allegations raises doubts about the authenticity of the interrogation minutes. Beria's wife Nino later refuted all these allegations forcefully, pointing out that her husband was a family man who attached great importance to a well-functioning family life, even more so during the war, when he had no time to indulge in such an immoral way of life at all. Only once during the war there had been disagreements and rows between the two, the reason being his constant absence from home due to the war effort. He worked day and night and was seldom seen at home. But the quarrel was later overcome.

Fourth: Beria was a permanent member of the State Defense Committee of the USSR during the war and responsible for evac-

---

[1] Ibid.

uations of industrial plants to the East, but also for munitions supplies to the Red Army, an extremely responsible position. He also played a leading role in organizing behind the front lines the Belorussian partisan war against the Nazis and their fascist allies. In 1944 he was appointed Stalin's deputy in the State Defense Committee, the supreme state body, and also received the marshal degree in recognition of his work by the Supreme Soviet. Was there time to have dozens of affairs in Moscow, to rape young girls, to kidnap them from the street, to abuse them and thereby risk his position? He was second in command in the Soviet hierarchy and had every interest in enhancing the moral authority of the highest state body in times of war.

Would Stalin, who was known to be an advocate of family values and an irreproachable way of life, have tolerated such a sex monster at his side? Beria never had a reputation to be thought-less, reckless, careless or to be a womanizer; on the contrary: He was known to be the exact opposite. And how could Beria have managed to keep all these affairs secret? Why would he ask his bodyguards to keep the lists? None of this makes any sense. We must therefore assume that the material collected by Rudenko and his deputy over half a year of efforts were fabrica-tions, intended to deal a mortal blow to Beria's high reputation in the Soviet population, but also in Georgia where he used to be First Secretary of the Georgian Communist Party.

Rudenko was later rewarded by Khrushchev for his work: In 1956 he was given the status of a candidate member of the Central Committee and in 1961 he became a member of it. During Khrushchev's time in office he condemned seven strike leaders to death. They had taken part in the protests in the South Russian city of Novocherkassk against rising prices. The protests were brutally crushed by the Soviet military sent in by Khrushchev and his government. Dozens of people died, among them some women.

For some who took part in Khrushchev's putsch against Beria and his Georgian collaborators, it was the start of a political career: A young army officer called Leonid Brezhnev stood guard in the Kremlin on June 26 during Beria's arrest. He later became General Secretary of the CPSU and President of the USSR. After

Rudenko's death in 1981, he was given a sumptuous state funeral to honor him for his loyal services under Khrushchev and also the Brezhnev regime.

e. Other voices

Even some Western observers admitted that the charges raised against Beria and his followers were a mere pretext for the judicial murder of Beria. Even Svetlana Alliluyeva, Stalin's daughter, who did not like Beria at all and who tended to believe every fake story that was detrimental to him, later said that

...Beria's trial was staged.., there was no evidence.[1]

So we know very little about the trial and what was said during the five days it lasted, as the documents have still not been declassified (allegedly 40 to 50 volumes all in all). And now that so much time has elapsed, these documents could also have been tampered with.

We only know who was condemned, who belonged to the special court, the wording of the indictment (treason, terrorism) and we know the verdict as well. We still don't know for sure whether Beria was even present in the courtroom or if an actor was used to replace him. We don't know when exactly he was liquidated: Some say on June 26, in his house, before the crucial Presidium meeting, others that he was executed following the December trial. But we do know that force was used to get rid of him and that high-ranking Soviet military officers, among them Zhukov and Moskalenko, played a decisive role in eliminating him. Zhukov first admitted it, but later he denied having been part of the operation — after he had been deposed by Khrushchev in the autumn of 1957. But one thing is certain: Without the assistance of Soviet top military brass, Beria and his Interior Ministry troops could not have been overcome. And even the Kremlin guards understood Beria could not have been overwhelmed.

Even in October 1952 at the 19th Congress of the CPSU, he was confirmed by the delegates in his leading position in the Presidium and Central Committee. That was the time when Stalin was still there. He also gave one of the key speeches at

---

[1] Svetlana Alliluyeva, *Twenty Letters to a Friend*, London, 1967, p. 375.

the Congress. In 1954, the readers of the Great Soviet Encyclopedia were ordered to remove the photos of him and all pages
mentioning his name and referring to him in a positive way. The
subscribers of the encyclopedia were asked to cut out Beria's
photos from edition no. 5 on pages 21, 22 and 23 by means of
a razor and to leave a margin to allow for substitute pages to
be pasted back in, pages which were then sent by the editors,
among them an article by F. W. Bergoltz and a series of photos
of Lake Bering.[1]

The author also mentions that immediately after the July
Plenum, which ended on July 7, 1953, a public campaign was
launched. All over the country meetings were organized to
"explain" to the Soviet population why this "enemy" was no
longer part of the Soviet leadership and could no longer be
seen in public. Newspapers carried banner headlines such as
these: *The Name of this Traitor will be Cursed for all Times, No Pardon
for Enemies!* Or: *The Dirty Plans of this Enemy Have Been Exposed*, etc.
(ibid.). At a meeting of the Defense Ministry, Marshal Bulganin,
later to become Khrushchev's Defense Minister and also Prime
Minister, gave a speech on the Beria case, and several Soviet
marshals, among them Zhukov and Sokolovsky, welcomed
his arrest. A resolution was passed that the Soviet army was
welcoming Beria's arrest[2] which shows again that the leadership
of Soviet military was highly interested and involved in Beria's
ouster.

Other Political Trials, 1954–1956

a. The trial against Abakumov and his MGB collaborators,
1954

Viktor Abakumov was the USSR's Minister for State Security
and head of the MGB, the forerunner of the KGB. Exactly one
year after Beria's trial, he is put on trial in Leningrad, the court
again is a military tribunal, and the trial is held behind closed
doors as well. The presiding judge is J. L. Zeidin who was one
of the judges of the Beria trial. Together with Abakumov, five

---

[1] Wolfgang Leonhard, Kreml ohne Stalin, Cologne and Berlin, 1963, p. 61.
[2] Ibid., p. 62.

other former collaborators of him who also worked in the MGB are charged with similar offenses: V. G. Leonov, former director of the Investigation Department of State Security for especially important cases; V. I. Komarov and M. T. Likhachev, his two deputies as well as I. A. Chernov and I. M. Browerman, two former employees of the Ministry of State Security. According to the daily newspapers *Pravda* and *Izvestia*, the five accused were charged with

...the same crimes that Beria has committed.[1]

Did they also rape numerous women if they committed the "same crimes as Beria did"? No, in this case these accusations are not made. Abakumov is also charged with having "fabricated the Leningrad affair."

The background: In 1948, Abakumov had Marshal Zhukov's dacha searched where great quantities of German war booty were found. After the war, Zhukov became head of the Soviet Military Administration in Berlin (SMAD), and in this capacity had ordered his underlings to steal valuables from the villas of rich Berliners which were subsequently put on trucks and brought to his Moscow dacha. Zhukov's dacha was found packed with valuable carpets, hunting rifles, porcelain vases and statuettes, precious paintings, books in beautiful bindings with gold embossing and the like by Abakumov's state security people[2].

Subsequently, Zhukov, the "hero of the Soviet Union" and liberator of Berlin in early 1945, was demoted by Stalin and sent to Odessa in a lesser capacity. But he escaped punishment in spite of his crime and was never charged with something for which ordinary Soviet soldiers were regularly shot during the war. Abakumov and Beria, however, had insisted on putting him on trial, but did not get their way for one reason or another. Reason enough for the marshal to take his revenge one day which he seems to have effectively done.

---

[1] William B. Bland, *Der Ärzteprozess and der Tod Stalins*, London, 1991, p. 76 of the German translation, quoting: *Aktueller Überblick über die sowjetische Presse*, Vol. 6, No. 49, p. 2, January 1955.

[2] Also see: Grover Furr, *Khrushchev Lied*, ibid., pp. 362ff, at: http://chss.montclair.edu/english/furr/research/zhukovtheft4648_var93.pdf.

b. The trial against Mikhail D. Ryumin, 1954

Mikhail Ryumin's execution was also decided in advance at a Plenum of the Central Committee of the CPSU as in Beria's case. He had prepared the trial against a group of Jewish doctors working at the Kremlin hospital who were accused of having spied for the United States and Great Britain (which one of them called V. N. Vinogradov admitted after his release from custody) and for having murdered high-ranking Soviet officials by administrating false treatments in order to cut short the lives of their patients, among them André Zhdanov and Aleksandr Shcherbakov, both close collaborators of Stalin. He was charged with having enforced false confessions and fabricated relevant court material. He spent fourteen months in prison after his arrest and was then condemned to death not on these charges, however, but on completely unrelated ones of having committed "economic sabotage." For the fabrication of evidence no death verdict could be pronounced according to Soviet penal law. He was a close collaborator of Stalin and led the State Security department for especially important cases.

Similar accusations against the Kremlin doctors were made by Marshal Ivan Konev the presiding judge in the Beria trial who had claimed in early 1953 that some Kremlin doctors wanted to kill him by a false treatment thereby contributing to the indictment of the doctors. But he was never charged with "fabricating evidence" as Ryumin was. Ryumin's superior, Semen D. Ignatiev, who was chiefly responsible for the arrest of the doctors, was spared prosecution and even readmitted to the Central Committee after his expulsion from the party. Ignatiev was close to Nikita Khrushchev. Ryumin was condemned to death after a trial lasting six days, whereas his superior was even promoted by Khrushchev and made First Secretary of the Autonomous Bashkiri ASSR. The trial against Ryumin was also held behind closed doors.

Obviously a close collaborator of Stalin who knew too much about what Khrushchev's people were up to was liquidated in order to silence him.

c. The Rapava–Rukhadze trial, 1955

In September 1955 the trial against Avksenty Rupava, the former Georgian Interior Minister, takes place. The presiding judge again is a military man: Major General Chertkiev. In the dock also is the ex-Minister for State Security in Georgia, Nikolai Rukhadze, plus six other former high Georgian officials who were active in the Georgian state security forces. They are charged with treason, terrorism and participation in counterrevolutionary organizations which are roughly the same charges made against Beria and his collaborators (Radio Tbilisi on November 22, 1955). The accused had been "accomplices of Beria," had allegedly taken part in his "intrigues" and were supposedly involved in "terrorist attacks" against a Georgian politician called Mamia Orakhelashvili and his wife. The latter belonged to the opposition in the Georgian Communist Party and was close to Khrushchev and his followers.

The verdict of the military tribunal: Rapava and Rukhadze are condemned to death by firing squad; the others get long prison sentences.

d. The trial against Bagirov, 1956

Bagirov was First Secretary of the Azerbaijani Communist Party between 1933 and 1953, a long-standing member of the Central Committee of the CPSU and a loyal supporter of Stalin and Beria. At the July Plenum where Beria was denounced and slandered by all the speakers, Bagirov had tried to save his skin by telling the new leaders that he fully supported the measures taken against "this rogue and international adventurist Beria".[1] He was tried only years later, in 1956, when after the 20th Congress of the CPSU in February 1956, Khrushchev's people had gained a broad majority in the Central Committee and Bagirov's own supporters were no longer there. Apart from him, five other "accomplices of Beria" were charged with treason, terrorism and activities in counterrevolutionary organizations — again the same standard charges as in the other cases. The trial took place in Baku, the capital of the Azerbaijani Soviet Socialist Republic. The judge put in charge at the military tribunal was A.

---

[1] Viktor Knoll and Lothar Kölm, eds., *Der Fall Berija*, ibid., p. 168.

A. Cheptzov. Bagirov was condemned to death and executed by firing squad. A plea for clemency made by the Supreme Soviet of the USSR was rejected by the judges.

e. Exchange of personnel

Soon after the July Plenum of 1953 where Beria was condemned, the leading personnel in the various Soviet socialist republics were changed to remove those who are not to the liking of the new power elite and their rulers:

> It was officially announced in Moscow on July 29 that Mr. Alexei Kleshev, Prime Minister of the Byelorussian Soviet Republic since 1948, had been relieved of his duties and succeeded by Mr. Kyrill Mazurov. At the same time it was announced that the Minister of Justice of the Moldavian Soviet Republic, Mr. Bondarenko, as well as the President of the Supreme Court of Moldavia, had been relieved of their functions and replaced by other officials. No reasons were given for the changes in Belarus and Moldavia.[1]

From this it follows that the Khrushchevites, who had now gained the upper hand in Moscow with the assistance of the leadership of the Soviet army, were not at all satisfied with purging the leading party bodies in the Moscow center but also wanted to get rid of all those irksome politicians who had shown in the past that they supported Stalin, Beria and their allies. A clean sweep had to be made everywhere to consolidate the positions won through the successful putsch in late June of 1953.

The purged politicians were then of course replaced by Khrushchev's own confidants and cronies. In those regions where Khrushchev's adversaries had a solid following, so-called trials were organized to get rid of them through "legal" channels, i.e., by using military tribunals for the purpose of liquidating "enemies of the party," "terrorists," "traitors," "counterrevolutionaries" and their "accomplices".

---

[1] *Keesing's Contemporary Archives*, ibid., p. 13,048, quoting *Le Monde*, Paris and the *Manchester Guardian*.

The Liquidation of the "Anti-Party Group" by Khrushchev and Zhukov, June 1957

In June 1957, at a meeting of the Presidium of the Communist Party of the Soviet Union, Khrushchev and his followers were losing their majority due to Khrushchev's continued mismanagement of the economy. The majority around Molotov, Malenkov and Kaganovich, later also joined by Voroshilov and some others, then tried to depose Khrushchev and to relegate him to the post of Minister for Agriculture. They proposed to make Bulganin First Secretary of the Presidium. The vote was democratically taken. Khrushchev lost and was demoted. What happened next?

Not much concerned about party rules and norms, Khrushchev, together with his followers, convened a CC Plenum to overrule the decision and to expel the group around Molotov from the party. Marshal Zhukov was helpful and, together with KGB chief Vladimir Serov, organized the immediate transport of the delegates who were known to be Khrushchev supporters. Candidates of the Central Committee who had no voting rights in such cases, were given the right to speak and to vote. Zhukov was only a CC candidate.

The vote was taken and Khrushchev's dismissal reversed. The "ringleaders," Molotov, Malenkov and Kaganovich, longtime collaborators of Stalin, were labelled an "Anti-Party-Group" and are later expelled from the party. Khrushchev remained First Secretary of the CPSU and succeeded in getting his people elected into the Presidium, where he now enjoyed a solid majority.

Molotov & Co., even though expelled from all party bodies, were sent into early retirement without being tried by a military tribunal, in recognition of the fact that all three had supported Khrushchev's plot against Beria and his followers. But now they themselves had become victims of Khrushchev's intrigues. Marshal Zhukov, Khrushchev's savior again, was then appointed Minister of the Defense of the Soviet Union in recognition of his swift reaction to Khrushchev's dismissal. In October 1957, Zhukov was removed from the newly-won post and from then on became an adversary of Khrushchev. He even defended Stalin in his memoirs.

A stenographic record was taken, but it is still classified and has not been released from the Russian archives. We therefore have to rely on what some witnesses have written about the Plenum.

a. Molotov's version

In the interviews he gave his biographer Felix Chuev in the seventies he was asked about the events and said:

> We were seven out of eleven, and his supporters were but three, including Mikoyan. We had no program to advance. Our only goal was to remove Khrushchev and have him appointed minister of agriculture...The Central Committee plenary session was held the following day...Zhukov is a great military man but a poor politician. He played a decisive role in elevating Khrushchev to a pedestal in 1957...We failed to have him removed as first secretary; we just didn't manage it. They convened a plenary session of the Central Committee, and the plenum sided with them — the game was over![1]

Molotov admits that his group did not have a "program to advance." So, to all intents and purposes, he did not criticize Khrushchev on matters of principle, but just wanted to have him demoted due to all the blunders he committed in the mid-fifties. He also supported his foreign policy of a rapprochement with US imperialism and Tito Yugoslavia. In 1949 Stalin had him removed as Foreign Minister and replaced him with Andrei Vyshinsky. Molotov also writes in his memoirs that Stalin had lost trust in him and refused to invite him to his inner circle.

Molotov had pledged the Crimean Peninsula to the Zionist Jews as a homeland — without telling Stalin anything about it — something which Stalin vehemently rejected; and Molotov wanted to give licenses to British papers and magazines to be published in Moscow.

---

[1] Albert Resis, ed., *Molotov Remembers*, ibid., pp. 354f.

b. Boris Ponomaryev (editor of the *History of the Communist Party of the Soviet Union*, Berlin, 1973)

> The Plenum of the Central Committee excluded V. M. Molotov, G. M. Malenkov and L. M. Kaganovich from the Central Committee and the Presidium...The Plenum declared that the activities of the Anti-Party-Group as being incompatible with the Leninist principles of the Party. In view of the irrefutable facts revealed at the Plenum, the members of the group admitted that they were guilty of having pursued harmful and factional activities and pledged to submit to the decisions of the Party.[1]

Only those members who were Khrushchev loyalists had been flown in to attend the Plenum of the CC, and they were also the ones who passed the resolution on the so-called Anti-Party-Group. Khrushchev had lost his majority in the highest party body, the Presidium, and could only be kept in power with the help of the Soviet military which was instrumental in getting the delegates loyal to Khrushchev to Moscow the very next day.

The event shows again that Khrushchev was none other than a stooge of the leadership of the Soviet army. All those who challenged the position of their man in power were immediately removed and pushed aside to clear the way for a completely new political course in the Soviet Union, a course which later led to the collapse of the USSR and to Boris Yeltsin's rule.

After his removal, the reformed Molotov radically changed his attitude towards Khrushchev: Now the former ally, who had done such a great job in liquidating Beria (Molotov in his memoirs: "...I believed, and I continue to believe, that this was to Khrushchev's great credit")[2] was called an "enemy" by him. Molotov now:

> He was a real foe of Marxism-Leninism, a real enemy of communist revolution, a covert, cunning, skillfully camouflaged enemy.[3]

---

[1] Ponomarjow, Boris N., et al, *Geschichte der Kommunistischen Partei der Sowjetunion*, Berlin, 1973, p. 714.

[2] *Molotov Remembers*, p. 345

[3] Albert Resis, ed., *Molotov Remembers*, ibid., p. 366.

And, surprise-surprise, the old Molotov seems to have also changed his attitude towards "the agent of imperialism," Lavrenti Beria, shortly before his death. In an interview with Literaturuli Sarkatvelo, published only three years after his death in 1989, he is quoted as saying that...

> Beria was a most clever man, inhumanly energetic and industrious. He could work for a week without sleep... As far as the accusations that Beria was an agent of a foreign country are concerned, they are untrue. He was loyal to the Soviet Union to a fault.[1]

---

[1] Amy Knight, *Beria. Stalin's First Lieutenant*, Princeton/New Jersey, 1993, p. 195.

PART TWO: ANALYSIS OF THE FACTS

Working Hypothesis for Further Analysis

After the successful October Revolution in 1917, the Bolshe-viks, led by Lenin, made an attempt to build a completely new society — socialism, the first stage of communism. The construction of socialism in one country surrounded by a great number of hostile capitalist nations could only be achieved by waging a class war against the old ruling classes that had domi-nated Russian social life for centuries. The fierce resistance of these classes, the landed aristocracy and the upcoming Russian bourgeoisie, was a logical outcome of the Socialist Revolution in October of 1917. The more successful Lenin and later Stalin became at building socialism in Russia in the twenties and thir-ties, the fiercer and the more determined the resistance of the former exploiting classes. After all, they were losing all they had, and they could only fight to turn back the clock of history and to reestablish capitalism.

This is one of the patterns that one can observe in the long run of history. Class struggle does exist; history can be seen as the history of class struggles; and if a formerly oppressed class, such as the working class or the poor peasantry, defeats the old classes in a revolution, the latter will never give up the struggle, to overthrow the revolutionaries, to reverse this event and to win back the upper hand. They will do everything possible to achieve that goal and will also turn to surrounding capitalist states for help to assist them in restoring the "good old order" of capitalism.

Talking about the situation in the Soviet Union, one cannot correctly assess the events in the early fifties which led to the ouster of Beria and other leading Bolsheviks without taking into account the class struggle. Under the Soviet system, the conflict between the working class and their allies, on the one hand, and the remnants and successors of the old bourgeoisie on the other, went on undiminished and even reached a new climax.

The defeated ruling class, the Russian aristocracy, had lost all its land as it was distributed to the people, and the Russian capitalists were dispossessed shortly after the October Revolution. Neither group was allowed to organize in parties and associations. They either had to leave the country by going into exile in France or somewhere else, or resign themselves to the new power relations; or they could resist by working clandestinely inside the Bolshevik Party or in other legal organizations like trade unions, youth organizations, the Red Army or the security forces, in an attempt to undermine these organizations from within. Some of them hoped one day to take over these institutions created by the Bolsheviks, with a view to transforming them into tools and agencies for the restoration of the old capitalist order. This was the only way of regaining power in the country.

Other ways and means had already failed, first during the Russian Civil War between 1918 and 1922 and later during the Great Patriotic War. In the first case, the principal capitalist countries invaded Soviet territory and sought to restore capitalism. Then, after the Nazi invasion in June 1941, Nazi Germany began privatizing manufacturing enterprises. As they rolled into the Soviet Union, German industrialists and financiers like Krupp AG and Deutsche Bank were beneficiaries of these efforts; but this attempt also failed.

In a third effort to roll back the revolution, anti-Communists worked to gain leading positions in the Soviet Communist Party by pretending to be staunch, 100% "Marxists-Leninists," hard-liners, dedicated "fighters for the working class," being more royal than the king and more Catholic than the pope, in order to gain trust and maneuver their way up the hierarchy.

Against this background I support the following hypothesis to understand and explain the events around Beria's and his followers' elimination from public life in the mid-fifties:

These were landmark events; they marked a decisive stage in the class struggle in the Soviet Union. They cannot have happened by accident, by dint of personal rivalries, or due to some ordinary power struggle within the leadership of the CPSU.

This class struggle raged within the Communist Party itself (still a hypothesis!), raged at the very top, in the Presidium of the CPSU between different forces who stood for completely different concepts and orientations for the future of the country. Beria was forcefully removed from the hierarchy because he was an obstacle to a Soviet counterrevolution led by Khrushchev and his supporters (especially in the Soviet armed forces). They sought to gradually dismantle the socialist system and especially the socialist economic system, which had been created under Lenin and Stalin, and to substitute it with an essentially capitalist system ruled by the profit principle and a privileged nomenclature. He had to be removed because he tried to do away with certain weaknesses and deformations of the Soviet system, among them the all-powerful "Communist" Party, to enable the Soviet population to play a more active role in constructing socialism in keeping with the Soviet constitution adopted in 1936, and to blow new life into Soviet socialism.

If we look at what Khrushchev and his followers actually did when they were in power, if we look at it over a longer period of time and from a principled Marxist point of view, we will perhaps realize that they were actually counter revolutionaries; and from the moment they were fully in power, they set to work undermining socialism according to a plan they had developed long before.

Faced with a functioning social and economic system supported by large sections of the Soviet population, they needed to do that under false claims of being "Communists," wanting to "modernize," "improve" and "humanize" socialism and to lead the USSR into a "glorious communist future," especially as concerns their boastful ringleader, Nikita Khrushchev. But what they said is not important, what is important is what they did and what effects that had. To achieve this goal, the last remnants of resistance, the last obstacles that remained after they poisoned Stalin, had to be overcome by force. This also is the reason why, up to this very day, Khrushchev is viewed positively in today's capitalist Russia and why he was also positively depicted by his Western biographers, among them William Taubman.

Beria, on the other hand, like Stalin, is still depicted in Western and also in Russian historiography as the prototype of a villain. His fight to rescue socialism and the proletarian dictatorship in the Soviet Union in the early fifties, especially after Stalin's violent death, has never been forgotten and is still a thorn in the side of the new Russian rulers. They are building a hybrid system with many capitalist features, and they downplay the Communist past. An indicator: In today's Russia, there are no official festivities to commemorate the October Revolution.

Up to this point, this is only a hypothesis and it needs to be confirmed by concrete evidence. If this is done properly, Beria's legacy must be newly evaluated, his person rehabilitated and viewed in completely new light, and people like Khrushchev also need to be revisited by anyone who wishes to be called an honest historian and not just a puppet of the state.

It will surely take a long time to set the record straight. Historiography serves a purpose: to legitimize existing power structures and to indoctrinate people with views and opinions which are supported and put forward by the exploiting classes and their agents in the mass media. Only from the grass roots can these false views be challenged.

The Main Charges Against Beria and Their Refutation

Up to now we've looked rather superficially at the facts and circumstances connected with Beria's liquidation. Now it is time to thoroughly examine the main charges made by his prosecutors and enemies in order to expose their substance. Rudenko, the Procurator-General, was appointed by Khrushchev. On December 23, the trial ended and Beria and his collaborators were shot by a firing squad. We may read that:

> The statement issued by the Procurator's Office said that the investigations into the case of Beria, "a betrayer of the motherland," had been completed, and that they had shown that "Beria, availing himself of his office, organized a treasonable group of conspirators...whose criminal aim was to utilize the organs of the Ministry of Internal Affairs...against the Communist Party and the Government of the USSR in the interests of foreign capital...and to place the Ministry of Internal Affairs above the party and the Government in order to seize power and liquidate the Soviet system with the aim of restoring capitalism and bringing back the rule of the bourgeoisie.[1]

This kind of charge is the kind we'll focus on, as claims of "moral depravity," with no hard evidence, are common tactics in character assassination. First they slander the person and the character of the politician to be destroyed, and after that the policy he stood for. Such allegations, unfounded, would go a long way to destroy the high regard in which Beria was held by the Soviet people, especially by the Georgians, and to also discredit the policies he had initiated shortly after Stalin's death. Khrushchev made similar charges against Stalin at the 20th Congress of the CPSU in early 1956 and at the 22nd Congress in 1961.

As Rudenko's charges to justify the death sentence against Beria had already been anticipated and brought forward at the July Plenum, I am now going to go into greater detail with the charges made by the accusing members of the Presidium and other members of the Central Committee.

---

[1] *Keesing's Contemporary Archives*, Bristol, 1952–1954, p. 13,363.

The first charge

> "Beria wanted to abandon socialism in East Germany. He
> was therefore an agent of the class enemy." (Molotov)

After Stalin's death, Beria managed to take charge of the
Soviet Ministry of the Interior. This does not mean that he was
not also interested in external matters, that he did not have
any foreign policy concepts and ideas, or that he did not have
influence on Soviet foreign policy at the time. As Deputy Prime
Minister of the USSR and as a member of the Presidium of the
Central Committee of the CPSU, he had considerable influence
to shape Soviet foreign policy, which he actually did quite effectively in the months leading up to his arrest (or murder) in late
June of 1953.

V. Molotov was acting Foreign Minister at the time, after a
four-year absence (Stalin had deposed him in 1949). Beria took
strong positions, especially with regard to the former German
Democratic Republic (founded in October 1949) and the crisis
that had emerged there at the beginning of the 1950s, but especially so in the summer of 1953, shortly before and after the June
17 rebellion of the East Germany working class.

Molotov to the delegates of the CC Plenum in July:

> When we discussed the German question in the
> Presidium of the Council of Ministers, we found that
> Beria's position was completely alien to the position of
> our party. At that time he said that it was not necessary
> to deal with the building of socialism in the GDR and
> that it would be sufficient if West and East Germany
> reunited as a peaceful, bourgeois state.[1]

Molotov concludes that Beria was a "defeatist" on the issue
of Germany (ibid., p. 79) and also that he was an "enemy of the
construction of communism in the Soviet Union." Molotov goes
on to say that...

> ...this man who throws in the towel and is a traitor like
> all the other traitors, with whom the party had dealt
> with previously, intended to return to capitalism.[2]

So, in his view, Beria must have been...

---

[1] Viktor Knoll and Lothar Kölm, eds., *Der Fall Berija*, ibid., p. 78.
[2] Ibid., pp. 81f.

...an agent of the enemy camp, an agent of capitalism.[1]

This accusation is then blown up out of all proportion and becomes one of the main charges in the later indictment serving to justify the death sentence against Beria.

To recapitulate Molotov's logic: As Beria held that building socialism in the German Democratic Republic was not essential, he must have been an enemy of communism in general, and therefore also an enemy of Soviet communism; and because he was such an enemy, he must be seen as a "class enemy" and an "agent of imperialism."

What exactly were Beria's views on Germany?

He did not write any articles or books on that issue. We can only tell from his actions as a member of the Council of Ministers what he thought and intended to do. We will completely ignore here the works of the writers of memoirs as the details they provide are contradictory and often of a polemic nature. There are at least two documents which can shed more light on his intentions:

First, let's look at what Walter Ulbricht, former leader of the GDR, called the "Beria Document" that talks about how to end the crisis in the GDR and the wave of emigration to the West in the early 1950s — a document adopted by the Council of Ministers of the USSR in late May of 1953 and also by the GDR leadership. Then we'll examine a second informative document: a telegram sent to the head of the Soviet Control Commission (SKK) in the GDR, General Chuikov, telling the Soviet military leadership in the GDR not to agree to the plans of the GDR leaders to close the border between East and West Berlin in March 1953 (see the documents in the appendix!).

a. The "Beria Document"

In May 1953, the Presidium of the Council of Ministers of the USSR (Beria was its deputy) met to discuss the worsening situation in the German Democratic Republic. In view of the wave of emigration of people from East Germany to West Germany, the Council of Ministers warned about the growing dissatisfaction of the GDR population with the leaders of the ruling Socialist

---

[1] Ibid., p. 83.

Unity Party (SED) and the state of the GDR. The document puts the blame squarely on the party leaders, above all, on Walter Ulbricht, the First Secretary of the Socialist Unity Party. Part of the document is a resolution entitled "Measures to Improve and Normalize the Political Situation in the GDR" signed by Georgi Malenkov, the acting Soviet Prime Minister at the time. There we read, among other things:

> As a result of the incorrect political line...there is serious dissatisfaction with the political and economic measures carried out by the GDR among the broad mass of the population, including the workers, peasants, and the intelligentsia. This finds its clearest expression in the mass flight of the residents of the GDR to West Germany...over the course of four months, in 1953 alone over 120,000. Many refugees are workers...It is remarkable that among those who have fled to West Germany in the course of the first four months of 1953, there are 2,718 members and candidates of the SED and 2,610 member of the Free German Youth.[1]

It is stressed that the SED leaders have been following ultra-leftist policies after the Second Conference of the SED in 1952 which are bluntly rejected as incorrect. The reasons given:

> The social-economic measures, which have been carried out...include: the forcible development of heavy industry, which also lacked raw materials; the sharp restriction of private initiative, which harmed the interests of a broad circle of small proprietors both in the city and in the country; the revocation of food ration cards from all private entrepreneurs and persons in the free professions; the hasty creation of agricultural cooperatives in the countryside in the absence of the necessary foundations led to: serious difficulties in the area of supplying the population with manufactured goods and foodstuffs; a sharp fall in the mark's exchange rate; the ruin of a large number of small entrepreneurs and artisans, of workers in domestic industries, and others.

---

[1] USSR Order 7576rs, at: http://ml-review.ca/aml/PAPER/AUGUST2003/ berlinBeria1953.html, p. 6.

It also set a significant stratum of the population against the existing authorities. This has gone so far that at present more than 500,000 hectares of land have been abandoned and neglected, and the thrifty German peasants, usually strongly tied to their property, have begun to abandon their land and move to West Germany en masse...All this creates a serious threat to the political stability of the German Democratic Republic.[1]

In order to correct the situation thus created, it was necessary:

to recognize the course of forced construction of socialism in the GDR, which was decided upon by the SED, as mistaken under the present conditions; ... to halt the artificial establishment of agricultural production cooperatives, which have proven not to be justified on a practical basis and which have caused discontent among the peasantry; to dissolve both those which were created on an involuntary basis as well as those which show themselves to be non-viable; ... to consider the policy of squeezing middle and small private capitalists a premature measure; ... to restore food ration cards to private entrepreneurs and persons of the free professions; ... to take measures to strengthen legality and guarantee the rights of democratic citizens; to abstain from the use of severe punitive measures which are not strictly necessary; to re-examine the files of repressed citizens with the intent of freeing persons who were put on trial on insufficient grounds; ... to assign special attention to political work among the intelligentsia in order to secure a turnabout by the core mass of the intelligentsia in the direction of active participation in the implementation of measures to strengthen the existing order.

At present and in the near future we need to put two tasks at the center of attention of the broad mass of the German people both in the GDR and in West Germany: the political struggle to re-establish the creation of a unified Germany and to conclude a peace treaty.

---

[1] Ibid.

At the same time it is crucial to correct and strengthen the political and economic situation in the GDR and to strengthen significantly the influence of the SED in the broad masses of workers and in other democratic strata of the city and the country; to consider the propaganda carried out lately about the necessity of the GDR's transition to socialism to be incorrect; ... to put a decisive end to the use of administrative methods in relation to the clergy; ... to put an end to the oppression of rank-and-file participants in the religious youth organization "Junge Gemeinde" (Young Community), moving the emphasis of gravity to political work among them...[1]

Finally, the goal of German reunification is emphasized:

...the main task in the struggle for the unification of Germany on a democratic and peace-loving basis..[2]

What conclusions can be drawn from the content of this document which, as we can assume, was drafted by none other than Beria himself on behalf of the Soviet Council of Ministers, which was the acting Soviet government?

1. Beria and the Council of Ministers did not want to give up the German Democratic Republic, not even the socialist beginnings in the late 1940s and early 1950s. He was worried about the loss of trust in the SED and advised the GDR leaders to do more effective work to win back this trust. Uppermost in his mind was to stabilize the situation in East Germany to halt mass emigration to West Germany which, in the long run, would have led to the collapse of the GDR. But he was clearly dissatisfied with the former leadership of the SED and their policy, and he wanted them to change course in order to win back the East German people's faith in the leadership. He saw that grave mistakes had been made (forced collectivization, hasty development of heavy industry, etc.) that had led to the crisis; and he felt that these mistakes,

---

[1] Ibid.
[2] Ibid.

first of all, had to be acknowledged by the GDR leaders before they could be reversed by initiating a new policy.

2. From the "Beria Document" we can also conclude that the goals of reunifying the two German states and concluding a peace treaty should not be given up. Beria followed in the tracks of Stalin, who was in favor of a neutral, democratic and peace-loving Germany on the basis of the agreements reached at the Potsdam Conference in July of 1945.

    Important to note, at that time plans had already been made in the West to divide Germany into two states, to integrate the Western state into the North Atlantic Treaty Organization (NATO), to militarize the country and to deploy imperialist troops on German soil to create a hotbed of tension in Central Europe with the aim of rolling back communism in Eastern Europe. The Soviet Union had a vested interest in preventing this from happening. It was vital to her security interests to create a united, neutral and peace-loving Germany to thwart the plans of the imperialists to start a new war against the USSR from European soil with the help of NATO.

What conclusion CANNOT be drawn from the document? The conclusion that Beria was an enemy of socialism or even an enemy of communism in the Soviet Union.

So Molotov was completely disingenuous in asserting that Beria was an "agent of imperialism." Western imperialism at that time was interested in having two German states, not a strong, unified German state.

Stalin's diplomatic note of March 1952 calling to organize free all-German elections, to conclude a peace treaty immediately with a united Germany, and to not allow German remilitarization, renazification and its integration into NATO, was immediately rejected by the West and its puppet, Adenauer's government in West Germany.

How can Beria be called an "agent of imperialism" if he put forward something that safeguarded Soviet interests and that

ran counter to the interests of US, British, and French imperialism? Drawing this conclusion is simply absurd.

b. Instructions to the Soviet representatives in East Berlin

Dated March 18, 1953, this second document was also apparently drafted by Beria in the Council of Ministers. It contains
instructions to the Soviet representatives in East Berlin, Chuikov
and Semyonov, not to give in to plans of the East German government to close the border between East and West Berlin, but to
reject them. The main points of the directive are these:

Top secret

To Cdes. Chuikov, Semyonov

Regarding nos. 8/1517 and 8/1543.

The proposal of the GDR leadership supported by you,
on the implementation of border protection guards on
the sector border of East Berlin with West Berlin and
on measures connected with the carrying out of such
protection, including the regulation of transport, appear,
in terms of political considerations, is unacceptable and
grossly simplistic.

Meet with Grotewohl and Ulbricht and tactfully explain
to them the following:

a. Carrying out such measures in Berlin with a population of several million people would certainly lead to a
violation of the established order of the city's life, would
cause the disorganization of the city's economy, and even
more would negatively affect the interests of the population not only of West but also of East Berlin, and would
evoke bitterness and dissatisfaction from Berliners with
regard to the government of the GDR and the Soviet
forces in Germany, which would be used by the three
Western powers against the interests of the GDR and
the USSR.

b. To carry out such measures with regard to West
Berlin would place in doubt the sincerity of the policy of
the Soviet government and the GDR government, which
are actively and consistently supporting the unification

of Germany and the conclusion of a peace treaty with Germany, and would seriously damage the political successes we have achieved in West Germany as a result of the implementation of that just policy which answers the fundamental national interests of the German people.

c. The deployment of border guards on the sector border of East Berlin would only complicate, to the clear disadvantage of the countries of the camp of peace and democracy, the relations of the Soviet Union with the USA, England and France, a development we can and must avoid.

...

From this, it follows that you must very seriously rethink this question and those practical measures which it is necessary to undertake in Berlin. We hope that you will look into this matter again more attentively in the next two or three weeks and give us your thoughts on this question.[1]

What conclusions can be drawn from this document with regard to Beria's stance on East Germany?

1. He was strictly against creating a pretext for the three Western powers to whip up tensions in the center of Berlin, which would have served their purposes to create dissatisfaction among the East Germans and to mobilize especially the Berliners against both the GDR government and the Soviet armed forces in Berlin;

2. He was in favor of normalizing life for Berliners, to ease tensions in and around Berlin and to continue Stalin's policy of cooperation with the Western powers to avoid a Cold War between the West and the East even at that early stage.

We know today that the warmongers in Washington D.C. and in London needed tensions and the Cold War in order to divide Germany, to deploy their troops and military hardware in West Germany permanently. Their strategy would have been served well if East German border guards had been deployed at the sector border in Berlin as planned by the SED leaders who feared losing control over their own population.

---

[1] At: http://digitalarchive.wilsoncenter.org/document/111327.

Later, in the summer of 1961, they did finally implement the disastrous, divisive plan and built the Berlin Wall to halt the wave of emigration to the West. This led to forty years of a divided Germany, and indeed, the GDR collapsed.

If moving to avert a disastrous division were the policy of an "agent of imperialism," then Stalin, who followed the same line, was also an "agent of imperialism." That would mean that the policy of implementing the Potsdam agreements and treating Germany as a single entity, of uniting the two parts and concluding a peace treaty with the government of a freely elected and united Germany, of creating a demilitarized zone in the center of Europe and a neutral, peaceful Germany, to give Germany an international status similar to that of Austria or Finland, would also have been a "pro-imperialist policy," which again proves to be completely absurd.

Molotov was the third speaker at the July Plenum in 1953 condemning Beria (Malenkov was the first and Khrushchev the second). He later told his biographer that he had this in mind when denouncing his former comrade, who was sitting in a military bunker and could not defend himself:

> Someone apparently suggested that Beria's conduct had to be discussed, and I was the first to speak. I said that Beria was a degenerate, that he could not be taken seriously, and that he was no communist. Perhaps he was, at some time in the past, but he was a degenerate now, and alien to the party. That was the essence of my remarks. I did not know Beria's past well. I had just heard some rumors and all kinds of talk.[1]

Can a politician like Molotov be taken seriously when he admittedly based his judgments on rumors? Anyway: his resentment of Beria made him an ally of the Khrushchev people who wanted to take over the party and to remove the last obstacle to achieve this goal after they had poisoned Stalin in early March, something which they themselves have admitted and which has meanwhile been proven.

So to sum it up: The first charge against Beria — that he wanted to give up socialism in the GDR and was therefore an

---

[1] Albert Resis, ed., *Molotov Remembers*, ibid., p. 344.

"agent of imperialism" — does not hold water. Beria stood in the best traditions of Soviet foreign policy to preserve peace in Central Europe and to thereby serve the vital interests of the socialist Soviet Union which had been the primary victim of fascism and militarism in the 1940s. The Soviet Union was vitally interested in a stable peace in Central Europe and at its borders. It was not vitally interested in a socialist Germany.

The second charge

> "Beria denied the leading role of the party. He wanted to establish his own dictatorship via the MVD." (Khrushchev)

The second most important charge against Beria was that he denied the leading role of the party in Soviet society and that he wanted to impose his "own dictatorship" by making use of his influence within the security apparatus, MVD for short, whose head he was at the time as Minister for Internal Affairs[1]. It was Khrushchev who made that point, saying:

> Beria tried to use the MVD for criminal purposes. By using the MVD, he tried to place the MVD above the party.[2]

To back up this claim, he said this:

> At that time, Beria said contemptuously: "Why the Central Committee? The Council of Ministers should decide everything, the Central Committee should rather deal with cadres and propaganda." I was dumbfounded to hear that. That would have meant to deny the leading role of the party and to reduce its role to the work with cadres (and this also only temporarily) and to propaganda. Is this a Marxist-Leninist view of the party? Have Lenin and Stalin taught us to have such an attitude towards the party? Beria's ideas about the party do not differ at all from Hitler's ideas.[3]

So Khrushchev asserted that Beria was a hidden Nazi, a fascist — a view which was then also reiterated by other speakers at the

---

[1] See minutes of the July Plenum, in: Viktor Knoll and Lother Kölm, ibid., pp. 52, 53 and 56

[2] Viktor Knoll and Lothar Kölm, *Der Fall Berija*, ibid., p. 53.

[3] Ibid., p. 56.

plenum, among them Lazar Kaganovich, who spoke later. Inter-estingly enough, Khrushchev, who later also condemned Stalin and called him all sorts of names (terrorist, dogmatist, dictator who neglected the party, etc.), at this juncture still refers to him as "our teacher" to make his point.

Let us now deal in greater detail with these accusations:

In his speech, Khrushchev did not provide any evidence for the charge that Beria intended to place the MVD, the troops of the Interior Ministry, above the party, and to thereby estab-lish his "own dictatorship." Neither did other speakers who repeated this allegation in their speeches, among them the new Khrushchev-appointed party leader for the Ukraine, Alexei I. Kirichenko. The speaker Mikoyan even repeated what Beria had once told him about the role of the secret service NKVD (the forerunner of the MVD). Mikoyan asked Beria why he still needed the organization and Beria replied by saying this (Mikoyan's words):

> Legality in the country must be re-established, such a situation cannot be tolerated any longer. We have many arrested people who should be released; people should not be sent to camps for no reason; the NKVD needs to be reined in; we are being spied on but not protected. This should be changed...[1]

So one of the accusers had to admit that Beria was in favor of curtailing the security apparatus, which runs counter to the accusation that he wanted to increase its role, and in 1939 when he had become the new head of the NKVD, he released more than one hundred thousand camp and prison inmates and reha-bilitated them, as has already been stated above.

But what about the charge that he wanted to deprive the CPSU, the only party allowed in the USSR at the time, of power and to reduce its role to propaganda and the selection of offi-cials? There is some evidence that he really did intend to do so during his time in office after Stalin's death. If he wanted to reduce the power of the Communist Party over the society, how "dictatorial" was that?

---

[1] Ibid., p. 214, excerpt from A. Mikoyan's speech at the July Plenum.

At Stalin's funeral in early March 1953, Beria was one of the official speakers. Mikoyan later referred to his speech this way:

> After he had made his speech in Red Square at Comrade Stalin's coffin, I said to him: "In your speech there is a passage where you said that the constitutional rights of the each citizen are guaranteed. If this was a speech of such and such a politician, we would assume that it was just meant to be a political declaration, but that coming from a Minister of the Interior, it's an action program, and you'll have to implement it." And he answered: "And I shall implement it!"[1]

In the same speech he said:

> The workers, the collective farmers, the intelligentsia of our country can live in peace and be confident, because they are aware of the fact that the Soviet government conscientiously and untiringly guarantees the rights which have been laid down in the Stalinist constitution.[2]

Significantly, Beria in his speech at Stalin's funeral only mentions the Soviet government, not the party. Here is a comment by a researcher by the name of I. Muchin:

> The ordinary people hardly understood what Beria said. For the party nomenclature, however, this was a heavy blow. Beria intended to speed up the development of the country without the party, i.e., without them. He promised to safeguard the people's rights which had not been granted by the party but by the constitution![3]

What does the "Stalinist" constitution tell us about the highest organs of state power in the USSR? Was the Communist Party mentioned as the highest organ of the state? Article 30 of the constitution of 1936, which was still in force in 1953, says explicitly:

> Article 30: The highest organ of state power of the USSR is the Supreme Soviet of the USSR.[4]

---

[1] Ibid., pp. 214f.

[2] At: http://msuweb.montclair.edu/~furrg/research/translations/stalin_demok_1. html, translated back into English as original could not be found.

[3] Ibid., Furr citing I. Muchin, *Ubiistwa stalina I beria, The Murder of Stalin and Beria,* Moscow, 2003.

[4] The New Constitution of 1936 (complete text, with a summary setting forth the Rights of Man), in: Sydney & Beatrice Webb, *Soviet Communism: A New*

So much for the legislative power. In Article 64 the executive and administrative organ of Soviet state power is mentioned:

> Article 64: The highest executive and administrative organ of state power of the Union of Soviet Socialist Republics shall be the Council of Peoples' Commissars of the USSR.[1]

The Council of Peoples' Commissars was later called "Council of Ministers." In fact, the Communist Party is not even mentioned in the constitution of 1936, which was drafted by a commission consisting of more than 30 experts. Stalin headed the commission and played a leading role in drafting the text. After that, the draft was returned to the country for discussion lasting more than half a year. Numerous amendments and proposals formulated by ordinary people were added to the text and approved by acclamation at the meeting of the Constitutional Assembly in late 1936, also presided over by Stalin.

For the first time, the rights of the citizens were given broad space in the text. The earlier constitutions had no list of "basic rights and duties." The right to work was included for the first time, but also other rights such as the right to rest and to material security, and the inviolability of homes and secrecy of correspondence.

Beria promised to honor these commitments in his speech, which seemed to worry Mikoyan, the closest ally of Nikita Khrushchev.

At the official May Day demonstration on May 1, 1953, when Beria was still alive and the most active member of the Council of Ministers (i.e., the Soviet government), banners were carried by people with the slogan written on them:

> The Rights of the Soviet Citizens Guaranteed by the Constitution are Unalterable and are Protected by the Soviet Government![2]

So Beria dealt a heavy blow to the nomenclature of the Communist Party, especially to the powerful party bosses of the

---

Civilisation, Vol. 1, 2nd edition, London, New York, Toronto, 1941, p. 528,7.
[1] Ibid., p. 528,13.
[2] Wolfgang Leonhard, *Kreml ohne Stalin*, ibid., p. 52.

provinces who were automatically given seats in the Central Committee.

They also feared the election system introduced by the Constitution, according to which secret votes had to be taken at all levels in all organs of power, and more than one candidate had to be proposed to the electorate. They wanted to be sure to be reelected, and Beria's stubborn insistence on these constitu-tional rules and regulations and his promise to put them into practice must have caused them headaches and sleepless nights. These worries are reflected in the speeches of some high party bosses, among them Lazar Kaganovich, who said this about Beria at the crucial July Plenum:

> For us the Party is the highest good. Not just once, the rogue Beria said this: The Central Committee should only deal with propaganda and partly also with cadres. To this he wanted to restrict the role of the Central Committee. But for us, the old Bolsheviks, the Central Committee constitutes the political, economic and party leadership of the entire life of the party, the country, and the state.[1]

Kaganovich then vented his anger by using a whole series of swearwords, calling him a rogue, a fascist putschist, a potato thief who had robbed the Soviet people of their potatoes by interfering in agricultural policies, etc.

In his book on his father, Sergo Beria touches on this problem, saying that his father was deeply concerned about the state of the Party and that reform was imperative:

> My father declared straight out, even in the presence of important cadres, that reform should have been under-taken immediately after the war, and even earlier. The Party had become a superstructure that accomplished nothing concrete yet controlled everything and involved itself in everything being responsible for nothing. He did not use these terms, but the sense of what he said went even further. I heard him expound his idea to Malenkov and he also spoke about it to Stalin. When he told Stalin that intrigues flourished in the Party because its members had no real occupation, Stalin did

---

[1] Viktor Knoll and Lothar Kölm, *Der Fall Berija*, ibid., p. 155.

not contradict him...In my father's view the country's leaders should feel responsible and the economy should be managed by people trained for that task. In no other state could one find a system in which decisions were taken by one group of people and carried out by another group, who were held responsible for those decisions.

The Party imposed decisions on the Council of Ministers and gave them the force of law. The ministers were mere executives, yet they bore responsibility.[1]

Beria proposed to implement the constitution of 1936 where it says in Article 3 in no uncertain terms:

All power in the USSR belongs to the working people of town and country as represented by soviets of working people's deputies.[2]

And in Article 94 these soviets are described as the real organs of state power in the whole country:

Soviets of working people's deputies shall be the organs of state power in the territories, provinces, autonomous provinces, regions, districts, cities and rural localities.[3]

This constitution was grossly violated during the "Great Terror" and remained merely a declaration of good intentions even after the war, which also made it imperative to reduce the role of the CPSU to its core functions: ideological work and the raising of politically qualified cadres. This was not an end in itself but would provide the economy and the whole society with highly qualified and capable leaders and activists. Beria's frankness and openness described by his son put the conspirators around Khrushchev and his followers on high alert. They realized that if Beria got the top job in the country, they would lose all the influence they had worked for so untiringly by moving their way up in the Party over the years.

Khrushchev was the ringleader of the bureaucrats, the local party bosses who ruled their oblasts (provinces) like little fiefdoms and detested the Soviet constitution and the soviets. They had also been the ones who initiated the "Great Terror" in the

---

[1] Sergo Beria, *Beria. My Father*, ibid., pp. 295f.
[2] Sydney & Beatrice Webb, *Soviet Communism: A New Civilisation*, ibid., p. 528,2.
[3] Ibid., p. 528, 18.

late 1930s to get rid of those people who wanted to implement the Soviet constitution of 1936, who were then called "enemies of the people."

Khrushchev, who accused Beria of wanting to establish his own dictatorship[1], harbored his own views about the meaning of real democracy. Later, the famous film director Mikhail Romm quoted Khrushchev at a meeting with intellectuals as saying:

> Of course, everybody has heard what you've said, and they have been talking to you. But who will decide? In our country the people must decide, and the people — who is that? That's the Party; and the Party, who is that? We are the Party. That means that we are going to take the decisions. I am going to take the decisions! Understand!?[2]

After Stalin's death, Beria soon set to work to put his ideas into practice, and the main idea was to exclude the Party from interfering in the economy. Sergo Beria has said more:

> Thenceforth economic and foreign policy decisions were taken at ministerial level, whereas previously they had had to be approved by the Central Committee. The Central Committee's economic departments were abolished. The only supervising organ was now the Presidium. The Central Committee was, naturally, much displeased with all this, since it lost its imaginary control over the economy — imaginary because what control meant was mainly intrigues and dismissals. The whole Party apparatus hummed like a beehive. All that was left to it was ideology! The Party now had charge of education and culture only! It was, above all, the top of the Party pyramid that was aimed at. Later, it was alleged that my father wanted by this means to take power for himself.[3]

So Khrushchev was right! Beria really did want to deprive the Communist Party of its excessive powers and reduce its role to the ideology. And he set to work immediately to prevent the members of the Central Committee and the Party secretaries in the provinces from arbitrarily interfering in economic and agri-

---

[1] Viktor Knoll and Lothar Kölm, ibid., p. 53

[2] Sergei Alikhanov, *Bagash na britshke*, at: http://www.kontinent.org/art_view.asp?id=2020.

[3] Sergo Beria, *Beria. My Father*, ibid., p. 254.

cultural policies to the detriment of the country. But Khrushchev was wrong when he said that he wanted to establish his
dictatorship through the MVD, the security apparatus. Sergo
Beria tells us why:

> My father immediately formed a special section within
> the MVD. Its mission was to prepare dossiers of rehabili-
> tation, to rid the MVD of all its repressive functions, and
> to set up "think tanks" inside the ministry for working
> out national and economic policies and formulating
> recommendations to put before the Council of Minis-
> ters. He composed a series of notes on these points. He
> wanted to build a real Ministry of Internal Affairs which
> would no longer spend its time imprisoning or trapping
> people and blowing their brains out...The major reforms
> were to be ready for introduction at the beginning of
> 1954.
>
> My father also began to clear the decks in the intelli-
> gence sector. His aim was to get rid of all the incompe-
> tent Party functionaries with whom our services abroad
> were lumbered.[1]

So Beria had also in mind cutting down the MVD to its core
functions, not just to reform the Party. The accusation that he
intended to establish his own dictatorship by means of the
MVD was invented by the witch-hunters to justify the arrest of
the troublemaker. The day of reckoning had come to settle the
score with someone who had attempted to rid the top brass of
the Party bureaucrats of their privileges and sinecures.

The third charge

> "Beria was an agent of international imperialism." (Kaga-
> novich)

In the resolution passed by the Plenum of the Central
Committee of the CPSU on July 7, 1953, entitled "On Beria's
Criminal Hostile Activity against the Party and the State,"
which was unanimously adopted with no abstentions, we read
under Point 6:

---

[1] Ibid., pp. 254f.

> In this connection the Plenum of the CC considers it to be its duty to call the attention of the Party to the case of Beria who was exposed as an agent of imperialism by the Presidium of the CC.[1]

If one takes the trouble to read the various speeches made by the members of the highest party body, it turns out that not a single piece of evidence was put forward for the "exposure." How can one expose someone by simply stringing together swearwords, insults, assertions, insinuations or accusations? This is impossible. Mere differences of opinion in the Presidium with regard to the crisis in the German Democratic Republic in early 1953, to the situation in Lithuania or Yugoslavia, are said to be sufficient "proof" of Beria's activities as an "agent working for international intelligence" (Kaganovich) or "for the Americans" (Snieckus).

Let's first start with the Lithuanian delegate Snieckus. He said:

> For whom did Beria blow up the situation in Lithuania out of all proportion? Apparently for the Americans.[2]

Here is Snieckus' "evidence": He claims that Beria insisted upon having more Lithuanians in top positions of the Party and the state, instead of sending Moscow-based Russians down there. So he does not have any evidence whatsoever.

Let's move over to CC member Mikhailov. He said:

> The secretary of the party committee had been trying to contact Beria for months to tackle the problems of party work, but in vain. This shows again that this provocateur and agent of foreign secret services treated our party organization with contempt.[3]

Again: no evidence.

L. Kaganovich, a member of the Presidium, in his speech:

> He wanted to paralyze our cadres and turn them into softies to be able to rule alone and to carry out the planned fascist putsch on behalf of the Party...This is a hostile line, this is the line of foreign intelligence services

---

[1] Viktor Knoll and Lothar Kölm, *Der Fall Berija*, ibid., p. 333.
[2] Ibid., p. 179.
[3] Ibid., p. 236.

which are also the sponsors of the roguish traitor...Under the present international circumstances, it is impossible to imagine such adventurers without being connected to imperialist secret services...There is no question that Beria was linked to international imperialist intelligence as an agent and a spy...This person has not begun to work for the enemy in the last few months but, apparently, slipped into our Party as an agent a long time ago.[1]

Kaganovich presents the following "evidence" to support his claims: the draft of a letter written by Beria for the Yugoslav Interior Minister Rankovic suggesting a normalization of state relations with Tito's Yugoslavia, and an "oral proposal" he heard from him that socialism in the GDR was not necessary. That was all.

In old age, when he had long been removed by the Khrushchevites from any position of influence (in 1957, actually), Kaganovich obviously regretted having made all those allegations. He told an interviewer:

> I will say the following. They never gave us any documents establishing that Beria was connected to imperialist powers, that he was a spy, and so on. Neither I nor Molotov have ever seen such documents.[2]

But at that time, even without such documents and real proof, Kaganovich joined the crowd to slander his long-time comrade in the harshest terms, thus playing Khrushchev's game of lies and fabrications, which contributed to Beria's execution and also to that of his comrades.

Former member of the Presidium Andreyev made this statement at the July Plenum:

> But even what the Comrade members of the Presidium have told us now shows that he had worked out a plan up to the minutest detail to liquidate Soviet power in our country, which, of course, was not only thought up by himself but in keeping with the directions given by his sponsors.[3]

---

[1] Ibid., pp. 151, 157, 162.

[2] Grover Furr, *Khrushchev Lied*, ibid., pp. 376f, quoting Felix Chuev's interview with Kaganovich, in: *Tak govoril Kaganovich. Ispoved' Stalinsogo apostola*, Moscow, *Otechestvo*, 1992, p. 66.

[3] Viktor Knoll and Lothar Kölm, *Der Fall Berija*, ibid., p. 286.

Andrei A. Andreyev, a long-time member of the Politburo (Presidium) of the CPSU, who had to resign his post for health reasons (poor eyesight), based his judgment solely on what the previous speakers had said.

Tevosyan, an ordinary member of the Central Committee, said this:

> Comrade Khrushchev is absolutely right when speaking about Beria's shady past.[1]

Khrushchev had claimed that Beria had been working for the secret service of the Azerbaijani Mussavatists, a reactionary group that was closely linked to the British in the 1920s. He, too, blindly adhered to Khrushchev's remarks and repeated them in public to show his allegiance to him.

V. Molotov, long-time Soviet Foreign Minister and Prime Minister, said in his speech:

> We have, so far, no proof that Beria was a spy in foreign pay, but that is not what is essential. It is clear that he was in the pay of the bourgeoisie, that he tried to corrupt the leadership of the Bolshevik Party by inculcating alien habits and methods...He wanted to replace Marxism by Americanism...His anti-Soviet plans assumed support from the imperialist camp...because he could count only on support from enemies of the Soviet Union in order to seize power.[2]

Molotov does not need any proof that Beria was an agent of imperialism, a claim he later repeated in various interviews with his biographer Felix Chuev.

By the way: What kind of "Marxist" was Molotov, if he relied on hearsay and rumors in making his judgments? It is a cornerstone of Marxism to rely on solid evidence, facts and documents to find a solid basis for one's judgments.

Since no evidence existed proving that Beria was a spy or an agent of a hostile foreign power, something had to be cooked up. Khrushchev provided the "evidence." He brought up rumors which had already been made in the late thirties after Beria had been appointed head of the NKVD, suggesting that during his

---

[1] Ibid., p. 299.
[2] Sergo Beria, *Beria. My Father*, ibid., p. 366, note 30.

time in Azerbaijan as an active Bolshevik he had worked under cover for the Azerbaijani nationalist movement, the Mussava-tists, and their intelligence service. This charge was later used by the judge of the military tribunal and greatly contributed to the death sentence he received.

Khrushchev used the allegations made by a member of the Central Committee, Grigory N. Kaminsky, who claimed in the late thirties that Beria had been an asset of the Mussavatists in Azerbaijan. At that time Beria could prove that he had been sent to the nationalists to spy them out but not to spy for them.

Before Beria was allowed to become the successor of Nikolai Yezhov, the NKVD chief who initiated the mass repressions in the 1930s on behalf of Nazi Germany, Stalin set up a commission to look into Beria's past. Molotov, Kaganovich and Malenkov also belonged to that commission. Beria could prove that the Bolshevik Party in Transcaucasia had sent him to the Mussava-tists to spy out the organization and that his underground work there was highly valued by the Party. The American Beria biog-rapher Amy Knight writes on this point:

> The commission included CC Secretary Georgi Malenkov, Sovnarkom Chairman Viacheslav Molotov, USSR Procurator-General Andrei Vyshinsky, and Beria. According to Roy Medvedev, Kaganovich proposed that Beria be appointed a deputy chief of the NKVD so that he would have complete access to the materials needed for the investigation.[1]

Later Beria succeeded Yezhov, and Yezhov was tried for spying for Nazi Germany and for having initiated the mass repressions costing the lives of hundreds of thousands of innocent people. Yezhov, who made extensive confessions, was executed in 1941. Meanwhile the interrogation material on Yezhov's case has been partly declassified, but many court documents remain hidden.

Beria presented a letter written by a high Transcaucasian party official by the name of Pavlunovsky. He confirmed in his letter to Stalin dated June 1937 that, indeed, Beria had been sent into the Mussavatist secret service to collect information on them but not to spy for them. The members of the commission

---

[1] Amy Knight, *Beria. Stalin's First Lieutenant*, ibid., p. 88.

to look into Beria's past were satisfied, and it was Kaganovich himself, now one of the chief accusers at the July Plenum, who had recommended Beria for the post of head of the NKVD, if we can believe Amy Knight. In his own Party autobiography, Beria himself cites his underground work against the nationalists, as Grover Furr tells us:[1]

> From February 1919 to April 1920 while I was chairman of the Comm. cell of technical workers, under the direc-tion of senior comrades, I carried out several tasks of the area committee, and handled other cells as instructor. In the autumn of that same year 1919, I entered service in counterintelligence from the "Gummet" party, where I worked together with comrade Mussevi. In about 1920, after the murder of com. Mussevi, I left work in coun-terintelligence and worked in the Baku customs house.[2]

Here is an excerpt from Pavlunovsky's letter of June 1937, attesting that Beria had done underground work not for but AGAINST the Mussavatists and was highly regarded by his superiors for his party work:

> To the Secretary of the Central Committee of the ACP, b [the former name of the Bolshevik Party — author], Comrade Stalin concerning Beria.
>
> In 1926 I was assigned to Transcaucasia [Georgia, Armenia and Azerbaijan — author] as Chairman of the Transcaucasian GPU [the secret service — author]. Before my departure to Tbilisi Comrade Dzershinsky, Chairman of the OGPU, summoned me and informed me in a detailed way of the situation in Transcaucasia. Then he informed me that one of my aides in Trans-caucasia, Comrade Beria, had worked for the Mussavat counterintelligence during the Mussavat regime. I was not to allow this situation to confuse me in any way or to bias me against Comrade Beria, as Com. Beria had worked in their counterintelligence with the knowledge of responsible Transcaucasian comrades and that he, Dzershinsky, and Comrade Sergo Ordzhonikidze knew about this. Upon my arrival in Tbilisi about two months

---

[1] Khrushchev Lied (ibid., p. 110)
[2] Grover Furr, *Khrushchev Lied*, ibid., p. 380.

later I dropped in to see Comrade Sergo, and he told me everything Comrade Sergo Dzershinsky had informed me about Beria.

Com. Sergo Ordzhonikidze informed me that in fact Com. Beria had worked in the Mussavat counterintelligence, but he carried out this work upon the assignment of party workers, and that he, Com. Ordzhonididze, Com. Kirov, Com. Mikoyan, and Com. Nazaretian were well informed about this. For this reason I should relate to Com. Beria with full confidence and that he, Sergo Ordzhonikidze, completely trusted Beria...

Two years ago Com. Sergo for some reason said to me in a conversation: Do you know that Rightists [the Soviet opposition belonging to the bloc of Rightists and Trotskyites — author] and other such trash were trying, in their struggle against Com. Beria, to use the fact that he had worked with the Mussavat counterintelligence, but they would not be at all successful in this.

I asked Com. Sergo whether Com. Stalin was aware of this. Com. Sergo Ordzhonikidze replied that this was known to Com. Stalin and that he had spoken to Com. Stalin about it.

25 June 1937,

Candidate to the CC VPK, b, Pavlunovsky.[1]

Kaminsky, who brought up the allegations against Beria in the 1930s, again was removed from the Central Committee at the 18th Party Congress of the CPSU that took place in March 1939.

So Kaganovich, as a member of the commission looking into Beria's past, and Khrushchev as well, must have known full well that Beria had not been spying for the Azerbaijani nationalists but was conducting risky underground work against them. But now they used the old allegations made by Beria's enemies — who even in the 1920s wanted to get rid of him — to rectify the inconvenient circumstance that, as Molotov stated at the July

---

[1] Ibid., pp. 379F, referring to: Aleksei Toptygin, *Lavrentii Beria*, Moscow, 2005, pp. 11f.

Plenum, there was "no proof that Beria was a spy in foreign pay". Later, at the 20th Party Congress in 1956, Khrushchev repeated these claims, this time to lash out against Stalin. Meanwhile, Beria's diary has also been published. *Russia Today* has put excerpts on its website. There we find an interesting entry dated November 8, 1938. Beria writes:

> Nobody knows, but we've just survived the most difficult moment. There could have been a terrorist act at the demonstration (he refers to the official demonstration on the occasion of the 21st Anniversary of the October Revolution attended by all top party officials at the Lenin mausoleum, including Stalin — author). Convenient time; everyone at one place. Dagin [Israel Dagin, head of the NKVD's department responsible for personal security of government members; arrested in November 1938 for conspiracy and executed two years later — RT] and his boys could have taken the risk. Koba [Stalin's nickname — author] realized it, but there was no way to leave the mausoleum. I personally controlled it all. Now it will be easier. I believe we have busted the most dangerous cell.[1]

Beria foiled an attempted coup d'état organized by Nikolai Yezhov and his followers. In the interrogation files on Yezhov's case we learn more about the attempted putsch which was coordinated with the German General Koestring, the military attaché at Nazi Germany's Moscow embassy. Yezhov admitted to having been a German spy since the early 1930s (recruited 1934 by German intelligence) and to being responsible for the mass murders in 1937/1938. Khrushchev later referred to him as...

> busy and reliable. I knew he was a worker from Petrograd, Party member since 1918 which recommended him to me.[2]

Khrushchev obviously sympathized with the Soviet opposition leader, Nikolai Yezhov, who organized the coup attempt in 1938, as he states in the interrogation files released by the Russian Federation. Beria foiled the attempt to murder the

---

[1] Excerpts from Beria's diary published on 22 April 2011 by *Russia Today*, April 22, 2011, at: www.rt.com/news/berias-diary-stalin-cried/
[2] Strobe Talbott, ed., *Chruschtschow erinnert sich*, Reinbek/Hamburg 1992, p. 99.

key Party leaders at the demonstration on November 8 and to seize power. Now the Soviet opposition headed by Khrushchev took their revenge, and the man who prevented them from taking power in the late thirties and who made sure that all the conspirators and terrorists were arrested and later executed, was himself arrested and called "an agent of international imperialism" — a way of indicating to the Soviet general public that his arrest was perfectly in order and a necessary step against an "agent of international imperialism"!

And there was another thing that must have sent shock waves into the camp of the Khrushchevites, and the hive was humming again. Sergo Beria in his book on his father:

> He wanted to establish the responsibility of every member of the Politburo and to be able to explain to the country how such things could have happened (referring to the mass repressions in the late thirties — author). The Party would then have taken decisions accordingly. Such a congress should analyze the whole history of the repressions...[1]

One of the first to stop him from doing that was Molotov, who asked him if he wanted them to engage in Chinese-style self-criticism. Beria denied that, but he insisted on convening an enlarged plenum of the Central Committee nevertheless to settle the matter, not by a vote of the Presidium but by a larger assembly. The plenum was to have been held in November or December 1953, Sergo Beria tells us. Beria's wife Nino's reaction when she heard her husband say this:

> Believe me, you've just signed your own death warrant.[2]

Wise words indeed! The plenum was convened, but not to shed light on the real perpetrators of the repressions. On the contrary: to eliminate the man who wanted to shed this light on the events in the late thirties, events, he himself put an end to in 1939 when he stopped the mass terror and released more than one hundred thousands inmates of camps and prisons (also see the document in the appendix).

---

[1] Sergo Beria, *Beria. My Father*, ibid., p. 258.
[2] Ibid.

Beria must have known many things about the role of some people at that time, and especially about Khrushchev's role in the mass murders as chief of the Moscow Party organization in 1937 and later as First Secretary of the Ukrainian Communist Party. The former chairman of the Moscow Soviet in 1939–1945, V. P. Pronin, in an interview with *Voenno-Istorichesky Zhurnal* (Military-Historical Journal) No. 10, 1991, had this to say:

> Question: And Khrushchev? What memories remain with you about him?

> Pronin:...He actively aided the repressions. A sword of Damocles hung above his head. In 1920 Khrushchev had voted for the Trotskyite position, and therefore, obviously, he feared the consequences, and he himself "battled" with especial zeal against carelessness, loss of political alertness, political blindness, etc. Khrushchev sanctioned the repressions of a large number of Party and Soviet workers. Under him almost all of the 23 secretaries of the city raikoms (city districts — author) were arrested, and almost all the secretaries of the raikoms of the Moscow province. All the secretaries of the Moscow Committee and the Moscow City Committee of the Party were repressed: Katsenelenbogen, Margolin, Kogan, Korytniy; all the managers of the sections, including Khrushchev's own assistant...He was the only one in the Moscow Committee who remained unharmed.

> Question: Do you believe that the scale of the repressions in Moscow was Khrushchev's personal "contribution"?

> Pronin: To a significant degree. After the autumn of 1938, the arrival of Shcherbakov to the leadership of the Moscow City Committee, not one of the Party workers of the Moscow Soviet, the Moscow Party Committee, the Moscow City Party Committee, or the regional committees was repressed.[1]

In 1938, Khrushchev was removed from the leadership of the Moscow Party organization and sent to the Ukraine, where he continued with the repressions. His own biographer, William Taubman, who was favorably disposed towards Khrushchev,

---

[1] Grover Furr, *Khrushchev Lied*, ibid., pp. 250, 251.

conceded that the repressions in the Ukraine even accelerated after his arrival. His right hand there was Aleksandr I. Uspensky, a Yezhov loyalist, later to be arrrested and executed for his crimes. He worked in tandem with Khrushchev in the Ukraine, arresting and killing thousands.

> In 1938 alone, 106,119 people are said to have been arrested; between 1938 and 1940 the total was 165,565. According to Molotov, hardly objective but extremely well informed, Khrushchev "sent 54,000 people to the next world as a member of the Ukrainian troika." Khrushchev's speeches dripped venom, and at least one case has come to light in which he scrawled "Arrest" across the top of a document that doomed a high official of the Ukrainian Komsomol.[1]

Here we are getting to the root of the fear that befell many members of the Presidium and the Central Committee when Beria managed to climb to the top shortly after Stalin's death. At the July Plenum, when Beria was already out of the way and behind bars, thanks to Zhukov's unconstitutional and illegal action, they could breathe more freely. They vented the pent-up anger against Beria, who had almost managed to get at them again, as he did in November of 1938 when he foiled the plot against the Soviet government headed by Stalin. But this time he failed.

The fourth charge

"Beria set the nations against each other" (Kaganovich)

Kaganovich again acted as a henchman for Khrushchev and his people at the July Plenum by making yet another charge against his former comrade, whom he had known for decades, and the method chosen was exactly the same he had used for the other charges made against him: He just strung together a multitude of accusations and allegations without taking the trouble to provide any solid evidence whatsoever. Here is what he said in front of the delegates:

---

[1] William Taubman, *Khrushchev. The Man and his Era*, ibid., p. 116. The arrest figures for 1938–1940 are in a report to the CC by a Commission headed by A. Yakovlev, in: *Massovye repressy*, p. 127.

> For him as an adventurer it is most important to increase national tensions among the nationalities, to set one nation against the other, to destroy the friendship among the peoples, to inspire and activate nationalists of all shades and to draw the dissatisfied nationalist elements to his side for the purpose of recruiting cadres for the struggle against the Party and Soviet power.[1]

If one looks for evidence for these allegations, one has to also study the other speeches, where we find some clues for Kagan-ovich's accusations. Let's see what Molotov had to say:

> Here Beria caused especial havoc [referring to his national policy — author]. For example, he demanded the replacement of the First Secretary of the CC of the Communist Party of Belarus, Com. Patolichev, although no reasons existed for such a move. He also blew up the weaknesses of the national policy in West Ukraine out of all proportion. The same can be said about Lithuania.[2]

What Molotov does not tell us is that there was a reason for Patolichev's replacement: Moscow had sent him first to Ukraine and then to Belarus to head the Communist parties in these republics, which was in clear breach of the Leninist policy on nationalities. It had been a principle of the Leninist Soviet national policy for decades to make sure that all posts of First Secretaries in the Communist parties in the republics and other influential positions as well should be given to local people speaking the native language and not to Russian-speaking appointees from Moscow. The former Russian chauvinist prac-tice, used by the Russian tsars, had created deep resentment and unrest on the part of the nations belonging the Russian Empire. This practice was ended by Lenin's first government immedi-ately after the October Revolution.

Anastas Snieckus, a Lithuanian member of the Central Committee, also claimed that Beria's national policy was mistaken. Beria, he said, wanted to present himself as the "only custodian of the national policy," but at the same time he had to admit that "there are very few Lithuanians in some rural Party committees" and that the Party work to promote national cadres

---

[1] Viktor Knoll and Lothar Kölm, *Der Fall Berija*, ibid., p. 143.
[2] Ibid., p. 92.

"has been poor." But as a consequence of Beria's wrong national policy, "nationalist elements were now raising their heads." [1]

Let's hear what Beria's son had to say about his father's ideas about how to treat the non-Russian nationalities. Did he want to set one against the other or even break up the Soviet Union?

> I never heard my father say anything to suggest that he wanted to break up the Soviet federation. However, he considered that the national policy pursued up to that time was bad and that immediate changes were imperative. The republics had to be rid of their Russian "overseers" and ruled by local cadres. He proposed that the USSR be ruled by a Soviet, the presidency of which should be held for six months at a time, taking turns, by one of the heads of the republics. [2]

A bit further down, he writes that his father often criticized the practice by which Russians were given leading positions in the republics, which he saw as a continuation of the old tsarist policy when governors were sent out to rule the provinces by decrees:

> He wanted to move the center of gravity from Moscow to the republics without questioning the union...The Soviet federation had be be decentralized. Only defense, transport and foreign policy should remain the responsibilities of the central administration, while everything else would fall within the competence of the local authorities...He discussed these questions fairly frankly with Khrushchev and Malenkov. Those two rascals were not so foolish as to contradict him. [3]

Sergo Beria recalled a conversation he had with his father when the latter tried to explain to him how absurd it was when the First Secretary of the Communist Party in non-Russian-speaking republics were not fluent in the local language:

> One day he said to me: "Just think, the First Secretary of the Communist Party of Lithuania or Estonia doesn't

---

[1] See Viktor Knoll and Lothar Kölm, ibid., pp. 180, 183.
[2] Sergo Beria, *Beria. My Father*, ibid., p. 260.
[3] Ibid., pp. 294f.

even speak the local language and can express himself only in Russian. And that's the norm!"[1]

His father attached great importance to promoting local people, but above all to getting the best people into leading positions:

> We need competent people who stay in place whatever happens.[2]

On the other hand, Beria clearly saw the danger of nationalism for he himself as a Megrel Georgian had experienced it in his own country. In his article entitled "The Victory of the National Policy of Lenin and Stalin" (Moscow, 1936), he vigorously denounced Georgian nationalism:

> During the years between the victory of the October Socialist Revolution in Russia and the establishment of Soviet power in Georgia, the latter country suffered almost three years of the rule of the Menshevik nationalists...they betrayed and sold the Georgian people to the imperialists of the West...[3]

He also condemned the Azerbaijani and Armenian nationalists, the Mussavatists and Dashnaks:

> They [the Georgian nationalists — author] tore Georgia away from revolutionary Russia, and together with the Dashnak and Mussavatists of the Transcaucasus, converted it into a jumping-off ground for foreign intervention and bourgeois-whiteguard counterrevolution against the Soviet government...Together with the Dashnaks, they organized a blood-letting fratricidal war between the Georgians and the Armenians.[4]

All this ended, however, with the proletarian revolution in Georgia on February 25, 1921, he wrote. Beria also helped create the Transcaucasian Republic (a federation of Armenians, Georgians and Azerbaijanis established in the 1920s) with a view to putting an end to the struggle among the three nationalities which had been at each other's throats for centuries. So if one

---

[1] Ibid., p. 295.
[2] Ibid., p. 260.
[3] Lavrenti Beria, *The Victory of the National Policy of Lenin and Stalin*, p. 13, Moscow, 1936, Prism Key Press, New York, 2011.
[4] Ibid., p. 21.

looks objectively at Beria's development as a Bolshevik, one soon realizes that he was a staunch anti-nationalist and supported Stalin's national policy of self-rule.

The fifth charge

"Beria wanted to conspire with Tito" (Molotov)

Diplomatic relations had been broken off in October 1949 following the expulsion of Yugoslavia's Communist Party from Cominform, the new Communist International. Vyacheslav Molotov, the long-time Soviet Foreign Minister and Prime Minister, took the lead in leveling the charge against Beria at the July Plenum that he was now conspiring with Tito.

To back up his accusation, he quoted from a "draft of a letter addressed to Rankovic," the Yugoslav Minister for Internal Affairs at the time. The document was supposedly found in Beria's briefcase when he was arrested. According to other sources, it was discovered in his safe which was forced open after his arrest.

"Prosecutor" Molotov to the delegates:

> According to the plan hatched by him, a representative of the MVD in Yugoslavia was to hand over a letter in Belgrade to Rankovic containing Beria's views which are alien to our Party and Soviet power. The representative was given orders to meet with Rankovic and to tell him: "I'm using this occasion to send you the best wishes of Com. Beria." Furthermore, he was to say to him that Beria and his friends "were in favor of thoroughly improving and revising the current relations between the two countries" and that "in this connection Com. Beria requests you to inform Com. Tito personally, and if you and Com. Tito share this opinion, it would be useful to organize a friendly meeting of persons who have been authorized for the purpose."

> This letter showed that Beria wanted to establish close relations with "Com." Rankovic and "Com." Tito. However, Beria did not succeed in sending this letter to Yugoslavia. With the draft in his briefcase he was arrested.

So apparently Beria wanted to conspire with Rankovic and Tito, who were acting like enemies of the Soviet Union. Is it not clear that this letter, written without the government's knowledge, was yet another shameless attempt to stab the Soviet state in the back and openly serve the imperialist camp? This fact alone would be sufficient to draw the conclusion that Beria was an agent of the enemy camp, an agent of the class enemy.[1]

It is highly unlikely that Beria would have kept such an important and top secret document in his briefcase. It is more likely that the letter was fabricated and smuggled into his briefcase to "prove" that he was an "enemy" and could therefore be charged with treason. Later the letter was "found in his safe," another indicator that the whole affair was fabricated in order to have a pretext to take him before the military tribunal.

They also claimed that women's underwear had been found in the same safe in his office, as well as lists containing the addresses of countless ladies with whom he was said to have had sexual intercourse. In any event, Molotov did not consider himself too good to make such seemingly absurd allegations to smear a comrade with whom he had closely collaborated during the war time. The alleged "document" contributed greatly to Beria's later death sentence and was another nail in his coffin.

And if such a letter did indeed exist, how should it be understood? Let us assume for a moment that Beria really did want to normalize relations with Tito's Yugoslavia in 1953, at a time when NATO (founded in April 1949) was looking for new members and Yugoslavia, despite her close ties to Britain and the United States (Yugoslavia had received military aid from the US since 1950), still enjoyed relative independence of the Western camp. Wouldn't it have been sensible to normalize relations with a country which had been liberated by the Soviet army in 1944/45 and whose population was not at all hostile to Russia and the Soviet Union, above all as far as the Serbian population was concerned, to prevent the country from becoming a member of NATO and joining the Western camp? How could such an act be equated with doing the imperialist camp a service, as Molotov claimed?

---

[1] Viktor Knoll and Lothar Kölm, *Der Fall Berija*, ibid., pp. 82f.

Beria's son Sergo on the Yugoslav question:

> My father's second project in the sphere of foreign policy
> was to bring about reconciliation with Yugoslavia. He
> pointed out to his colleagues that Tito had not joined
> the Atlantic alliance in spite of the extremely difficult
> situation his country was in. He had held out...However,
> Molotov agreed with my father, and he was given the
> task of restoring ties with Belgrade, as he had retained
> networks in that country. He did that and reported that
> the Yugoslavs had agreed, for their part, to admit some of
> their own mistakes (purchasing arms from America), so
> that the Soviet leaders should not lose face completely.
> All that remained was to make this decision public.
>
> The text of the letter to Rankovic, which was attributed
> to my father, had received Molotov's approval.[1]

On June 15, 1953, two weeks before the crucial meeting of the
Presidium where, allegedly, Beria was arrested by Soviet military,
and three weeks before the July Plenum where Molotov made
his accusations, the Yugoslav leadership had already accepted a
Soviet proposal to normalize diplomatic relations:

> The Soviet proposal had been made on June 6 by Mr.
> Molotov to the Yugoslav chargé d'affaires in Moscow
> (Mr. Djuritch), following an earlier meeting between
> Mr. Molotov and Mr. Djuritch on April 29 — the first
> such meeting between a Soviet Foreign Minister and a
> Yugoslav envoy since the Soviet break with Yugoslavia
> in 1949.[2]

So Beria's proposals and ideas were nothing new; they corre-
sponded with the official government line and were not at all
"alien to our Party and Soviet power," as Molotov claimed.

Molotov was Foreign Minister at the time and remained in
that position until 1956. Apparently, he had agreed to normalize
relations with Yugoslavia. When Khrushchev (and Malenkov)
went to Belgrade in 1955 to meet with Tito, Molotov did not
resign but accepted the new official line of establishing normal
relations with Tito's Yugoslavia. If he had serious misgivings on

---

[1] Sergo Beria, *Beria. My Father*, ibid., p. 263.
[2] *Keesing's Contemporary Archives*, Vol. 9, covering the years 1952–1954, Bristol, p. 13,001.

that and thought it was "treasonable" and "served the enemy camp," etc., he should have resigned immediately to show his discontent and indicate that he did not want to be involved in such treasonable acts. But he did nothing of the kind.

If the letter did exist and was found in Beria's pocket or briefcase or in his safe or wherever, its content was in line with the official policy later adopted by the Khrushchev regime itself. How could such a letter have inflicted damage to the Soviet Union? What exactly did the damage consist of? If the step contributed to Yugoslavia not joining NATO, the way West Germany and Turkey did, it was surely a blessing and not a curse.

How could Molotov dare to act as a prosecutor in front of the delegates, when he himself had established contacts with the Yugoslav envoy only weeks before and when he had even approved of the letter, as Beria's son claims? Was he trying to save his own skin by making those allegations and to rescue his political career as foreign minister? Molotov, who was later (in the summer of 1957) himself called an "enemy" — not an enemy of the state but an "enemy of the Party" — by Khrushchev and his cronies, again shows that he did not have any backbone or principles. He joined the crowd to hunt Beria down and to get rid of him.

And what about Khrushchev himself? In 1953 he supported Molotov's allegations at the crucial July Plenum, yet after his visit to Yugoslavia in 1955 he declared that Beria and Abakumov had been the ones who had engineered the ending of diplomatic relations with Yugoslavia in the first place.[1] First Beria is accused of having engineered the normalization of relations with Yugoslavia, thereby qualifying as "an enemy of the Party and Soviet power," and later he is accused of having broken off the relations!

This shows again how eager, how desperate these people were to liquidate Beria by any means possible.

Further charges

Up to now we have dealt with the main charges, but there were other ones as well. It is not much use dealing with these

---

[1] (see Strobe Talbott, ed., *Chruschtschow erinnert sich*, ibid., p. 107, note 39

"minor" charges in detail, as they are to all intents and purposes absurd and polemical. They just show the anger and wrath of some delegates who considered Beria and his reform policy to be a threat.

Beria was also called a "saboteur" who had intervened in agricultural policies and had intended to "steal potatoes from the Soviet people"; he was accused of having initiated the release from labor camps and prisons of more than one million inmates, although the amnesty law had been signed by the Supreme Soviet, the highest legislative body in the USSR on March 28. Voroshilov, then Chairman of the Supreme Soviet, had proclaimed the law himself; now he used it against Beria. He was also charged with having forbidden the use of portraits of Soviet leaders at official demonstrations, to put an end to any kind of personality cult. Under Khrushchev this practice was reintroduced, although he himself later denounced the personality cult that developed under Stalin in his "Secret Speech." Ridiculous charges were made in connection with the book he had written in 1940 on the history of the Bolshevik organizations in Transcaucasia. This book, it was said, had not been written by himself but by a historian, with the aim of worming himself into Stalin's good graces and boosting his Party career. Someone said — without providing any evidence — that he had ordered the use of torture at interrogations and that he had tortured prisoners himself; that he had abused and raped numerous women and therefore was a "degenerate," and so on.

Beria's Reform Initiatives During His Interregnum

Having dealt with the main charges against Lavrenti Pavlovich Beria, we can safely say that the accusations made by the top brass of the Soviet hierarchy (excluding the marshals who were not present at the July meeting) were purely designed to prepare the indictment for his trial in December and, at the same time, to deflect attention from his chief reform initiatives launched during his short 112-day interregnum as Minister of the Interior and Deputy Head of the Soviet government.

These reform initiatives were numerous and clearly designed to exclude the Central Committee of the CPSU from interfering in the economy, including agriculture, in foreign policy issues, and, above all, they were meant to restore the Soviet constitution of 1936 ("All Power to the Soviets!"). If these reforms — scheduled for a longer period of time — had been put into effect, it would have meant putting an end to the omnipotence of the CPSU and its leading bodies and shifting the balance of power in the country towards the soviets, restoring people's power in the USSR and granting the numerous nationalities and peoples of the Soviet Union greater autonomy. It would have meant ending the prerogatives and privileges of the First Secretaries in the provinces and also taking steps to come to terms with the past, especially with the year 1937, the year of the repressions.

But one thing must be clarified from the start, to preempt a misunderstanding: Beria did not want a Gorbachev-style "perestroika." He did not envisage a complete overhaul of the Soviet economic system in order to restore a "free market economy," another term for capitalism. He was strictly against privatizing people's property and did not want to put an end to collectivization and to restore private ownership of land. He also wanted to preserve the Soviet Union and had absolutely no designs to destroy it and turn it into a "Community of Independent States." His reform concept was restricted to the political superstructure and was not designed to touch the healthy economic base of the Soviet Union.

This is a fundamental difference between "reformers" like Khrushchev, Gorbachev and Yeltsin, who were counterrevolutionaries and intended to restore capitalism in the Soviet Union, and a true reformer like Beria whose main concern was to free the Soviet Union from an all-powerful party apparatus and a nomenclature securely embedded in it and intent on fighting to preserve its many unearned privileges. These people often had no qualifications whatsoever and were often outright incompetent; maybe they were excellent orators, but they avoided responsibility at all costs and were also frequently involved in petty intrigues. Beria wanted to get rid of these many careerists and Party bosses who pretended to be "Communists" but were often only interested in their privileges.

Let's now take a look at Beria's most important reform initiatives.

a. "The Party should no longer decide everything"

Beria's son Sergo sums up his father's main preoccupation at
the time of his three-and-a-half-month interregnum (March till
the end of June 1953) this way:

> My father said that the old system was justified so long
> as there were still people who had been brought up
> under the tsarist regime and received a bourgeois educa-
> tion. But now, when we had already reached the third
> generation of Soviet people, we could not entrust the
> countries' administration to Party apparatchiks. They
> should confine themselves to activity in their cells. It
> was not up to the Central Committee to run the country;
> that was the job of the Council of Ministers. The experi-
> ence of the Soviet Union and of the other socialist coun-
> tries showed that the Party ought to devote itself exclu-
> sively to ideology, education and culture, to everything
> that went to form the new man, without interfering in
> the economy...

> "But here the Party decides everything, both harvests and
> arrests. Its leaders dominate everything and are respon-
> sible for nothing. What I want is for everybody hence-
> forth to be answerable for his actions."[1]

Khrushchev's American biographer, William Taubman)who
also writes about the Beria interregnum) confirms this:

> ...But the party's writ seemed reduced to propaganda and
> ideology, with political and economic matters left to
> Malenkov and Beria.[2]

Sergo Beria also writes that concrete steps were taken to put
this reform into effect and that Malenkov, then Prime Minister
and chairman of the Council of Ministers, and Khrushchev as
well, did not raise any objections to his plans. From now on all
important economic and foreign policy decisions were taken
at ministerial level and no longer needed to be approved by the

---

[1] Sergo Beria, *Beria. My Father*, ibid., p. 253.
[2] William Taubman, *Khrushchev. The Man and his Era*, ibid., p. 245.

Central Committee. So the CC's economic departments became obsolete and were disbanded, to the dismay of Khrushchev and his followers. Khrushchev quoted Beria as saying at the July Plenum:

> "What are you saying about the Central Committee? It is for the Council of Ministers to decide everything, and the Central Committee can busy itself with cadres and propaganda." This statement left me flabbergasted. It meant that Beria rejected the leading role of the Party...[1]

Khrushchev, as long as Beria was still around and the number two in the hierarchy (Khrushchev was just the Party's secretary and was not even a member of the government), never objected to anything he said and did, but kept his opinion to himself, causing Beria to think that he was an ally and not a mortal enemy. This made him think that he also had the support of the Party leadership, but in reality, things turned out to be quite different, and he paid a high price for his openness. The plotters used everything he said to them for their own purposes.

b. "Back to Stalin's Foreign Policy on Germany"

Stalin wanted a neutral, democratic, peaceful unified Germany in Central Europe and an implementation of the Potsdam Accords reached with his Western allies in Berlin in July/August 1945.

In March 1952 he sent a diplomatic note to the Western leaders and their ally in Bonn/West Germany, proposing immediate free and general elections, and after an all-German government was elected and in power, the negotiation of a peace treaty to be concluded with the new German government. Germany was to stay out of political and military alliances, should be allowed to have a reasonably equipped army of its own to defend itself, its borders should be those agreed upon at the Potsdam Conference, all foreign troops should leave Germany within a certain period of time, and the new Germany should also become a member of the United Nations and other international organizations.

---

[1] Sergo Beria, *Beria. My Father*, ibid., p. 364, note 5 for chapter 11.

Free elections in Germany would probably have brought a social-democratic government into power and would have meant the end of the German Democratic Republic and the unpopular Ulbricht-Grotewohl government in East Berlin, but also the end of the anti-Communist Adenauer regime in Bonn. This was the official line as long as Stalin lived, which was supported by Beria and the Soviet Council of Ministers before and after his death in 1953 — but not by Molotov and Khrushchev.

The main thing for the Soviet Union under Stalin was to prevent any new German aggression against the USSR. The Soviet government was primarily interested in having peaceful neighbors at its borders, not necessarily socialist ones. Stalin knew that the Germans in their majority did not want socialism; they had never wanted it, only a small minority had. He suspected that a socialist Germany was not viable in the long run. He once said: "Imposing socialism on Germans is like putting a saddle on a cow."

The Western powers immediately rejected his proposals and the draft peace treaty that was attached, as they feared that a neutral Germany would not join NATO and could become an important peaceful and internationally recognized trading partner for East and West, thus challenging the American monopolies and their economic strategy for Europe.

This neutral Germany could also become, if not an ally of the USSR, at least a partner when it came to preserving peace in Europe. However, according to the policy planners in Washington D.C. and London (Winston Churchill!), American and British forces were to stay in West Germany for good and the West German Bonn government, which was nothing but a puppet of the United States, was to become a NATO member. It was to have a powerful army led by former Nazi generals to serve their policy of "rolling back Communism" and to prepare for a new war against the USSR. Had they accepted Stalin's proposals, these plans would have come to nothing. But in favor of these plans there existed an overwhelming majority within the German population that had also suffered greatly under World War II. The powerful peace movement in the two German states, which emerged in the early 1950s, was proof of that.

Beria was in favor of pursuing this line even after Stalin's death, and it should be noted that at that time, the Federal Republic of Germany (West Germany) was not yet a member of NATO. It only joined the anti-Communist organization in 1954. So there was still a chance to reach an agreement to preserve the neutrality of the country, to give it a status like that of Austria or Finland, in keeping with the Potsdam Agreement which treated Germany as a whole.

Beria's son Sergo writes this with regard to his father's foreign policy ideas:

> My father returned to his idea of reunifying Germany. He argued for this by stressing that the United States would be kept busy for a long time with decolonizing the British Empire and the other colonial empires. While that was going on the German-Russian tandem would carry through an economic transformation. Reunified Germany would be grateful to the Soviet Union and would agree to help it economically. We would even put up with a bourgeois Germany.[1]

But at that time Molotov was Minister of the Foreign Affairs again. In 1949 Stalin had managed to depose him and to replace him with Andrei Vyshinsky. Shortly after the 19th Party Congress in October 1952 (Oct. 5–14) at the First Plenum of the Central Committee, in a motion carried by the majority, he managed to keep Molotov—and also Khrushchev's closest ally Mikoyan—out of the inner circle of the new and greatly enlarged Presidium, a small group of ten, formerly called the Politburo.

Molotov had suggested giving the Crimean Peninsula to the Zionist Jews as a homeland, which Stalin vigorously rejected. Molotov was reinstated as Foreign Minister while Stalin lay unconscious on his death bed in early March, by agreement of a majority of Presidium members who were gathered in an adjoining room. So Molotov was there again, and he had completely different ideas, which were supported by Khrushchev and his followers.

At the July Plenum, Khrushchev said this about Beria's "dangerous" foreign policy ideas:

---

[1] Ibid., p. 262.

When we discussed the German question, he clearly acted as a provocateur and as an agent of imperialism. He went so far as to openly propose abandonment of the building of socialism in East Germany...He said: "A neutral, democratic Germany must be created."[1]

These views were fully supported by Molotov, as we have already seen above. So according to Khrushchev, Beria and Stalin were "agents of imperialism."

Beria tried hard and used all his eloquence to win the other Presidium members back to Stalin's foreign policy on Germany, but he did not succeed. After Stalin's death important positions were now occupied by people who were diametrically opposed to these views and who favored two German states, thus playing into the hands of those in the West who wanted to use Germany as an occupied territory for their own strategic purposes.

c. "Amnesty for over one million people"

In late March, an amnesty law drafted by Beria was passed, releasing more than one million people from prison and labor camps. The law was promulgated by Kliment Voroshilov, the new official head of state, on March 27, 1953. All those who had been sentenced to prison or labor camp internment of less than five years were freed. Pregnant women, mothers with children, youth under the age of eighteen and inmates of old age were to be released immediately. The sentences of other convicted people were halved, with the exception of those who had been tried and convicted for counterrevolutionary crimes, murder, theft or embezzlement.[2]

Beria who, as we have seen, had pledged in his speech at Stalin's funeral to restore legality and the constitution, only needed three weeks to put his plans into practice. This is a reminder of what he did in 1939 after he became chairman of the NKVD: At that time he released more than one hundred thousand inmates and set up commissions to look into their cases

---

[1] Viktor Knoll and Lothar Kölm, *Der Fall Berija*, ibid., p. 66.
[2] Georg Paloczi-Horvath, Chruschtschow, Frankfurt/Main and Hamburg, 1961, p. 150

with a view to rehabilitating them. (also see document in the appendix!).

d. "A ban to be imposed on the displaying of portraits of leaders of the Party and the state"

Beria was a firm opponent of any kind of personality cult and initiated an order to ban all portraits of leaders at official demonstrations and festivities. Khrushchev, who would later denounce Stalin's personality cult that he himself had helped to create in the 1930s, was against the ban in 1953. Beria is reported to have said to him:

> "I look like an idiot in my pince-nez. And you look like a piglet. Does it give you pleasure to see yourself at every street corner?" he concluded, turning to Khrushchev. He also wanted to rename the innumerable places and enterprises that bore the names of our leaders. "In the United States a great president like Roosevelt hasn't even got a monument. We should copy them if we want to seem civilized." This charge was also laid against him, that he wanted to deprive the masses of the possibility of contemplating their guides.[1]

But on the other hand he proposed decorations honoring national heroes of the republics, which made him no friend of some Russian chauvinists within his party.

e. "The Jewish doctors given amnesty"

A number of Jewish Kremlin doctors, among them Stalin's own personal physician Vladimir Vinogradov, were accused of having murdered high-ranking Soviet politicians by prescribing wrong treatments with a view to cutting their lives short. Among the apparent victims were Aleksandr Shcherbakov, in May 1945, and Andrei Zhdanov, in the summer of 1948. Both died of sudden heart attacks in hospital. Shcherbakov, Khrushchev's successor as head of the Moscow Party organization, died at the age of 44 on May 9, 1945, when the doctors allowed him to leave the hospital despite a serious heart condition. A woman

---

[1] Sergo Beria, *Beria. My Father*, ibid., p. 256.

doctor named Lydia Timashuk, a radiologist, wrote a letter to Stalin telling him that Andrei Zhdanov, while staying in the hospital, also with a serious heart condition, had been given the wrong treatment by a group of physicians, some of them Jewish, but not all of them.

This set the ball rolling for an inquiry in the course of which more than a dozen physicians employed at the Kremlin hospital, nearly all of them professors but not all of them Jewish, were arrested and accused of working for a Zionist organization called JOINT which was seemingly used by Western embassies in Moscow for spying and other anti-Soviet purposes.

The man in charge of the investigation was M. Ryumin, who belonged to Stalin's own security network. The man bearing the overall responsibility for the arrest of the doctors was S. D. Ignatiev, who was close to Khrushchev and was distrusted by Beria.

On April 4, one month after Stalin's death, Beria as Minister of the Interior and chief of the MVD, the security apparatus, decided to set the doctors free without consulting his colleagues in the Party leadership, as he was apparently not convinced of their guilt and because he thought that illegal methods of extracting confessions had been used. He then ordered the arrest of Ignatiev. This decision was never revoked; the doctors were not rearrested after Beria's ouster but remained free and could continue their work in the hospital. Vinogradov later confessed that he had indeed been spying for France and Great Britain.[1]

We have reason to believe that Beria promised to set the doctors free in early March when Stalin fell ill and the leading positions in the Party and state were redistributed among the members of the Presidium, to get the other Presidium members to consent to Beria's being given the important Ministry of the Interior and thereby also control of the security apparatus. Beria's son Sergo, however, believes that he had other reasons to set them free. Once he overheard a conversation between his father and her mother on the issue. His father telling his wife Nino:

---

[1] Yakov Rapoport, *The Doctors' Plot. Stalin's Last Crime*, London, 1991, p. 138).

> "Have you still not understood that Khrushchev partici-
> pated in the anti-Semitic campaign [the campaign started
> against the Kremlin doctors in early 1953 — author] not
> because he was forced to by Stalin but because he is
> himself a furious anti-Semite?"[1]

So this may have been a wrong move on the part of Beria. Of
course, this decision was also turned against him at the July
Plenum.

f. "More legality"

Beria, who was accused of establishing his own private dictatorship with the help of the MVD, introduced important steps
to curtail the powers of the security apparatus and to end the
practice of condemning people to long prison or labor camp
sentences by special MVD commissions. But he was not in a
position to close down all special tribunals, among them the
military ones, one of which would later condemn him to death.
Beria's son:

> He had the investigation department of the MVD and
> the Gulag transferred to the Ministry of Justice. He had
> always been against the inclusion of these administra-
> tions in the MVD.[2]

This measure was taken on March 28 by the Council of
Ministers, on Beria's initiative. The Gulag ruled by the NKVD
and later by the MVD, the successor organization, was now no
longer controlled by the security service but by official government bodies. The Soviet deep state suffered a severe blow, at least
for the time being. After his arrest the measure was declared null
and void.

He also gave instructions to set up a committee to rehabilitate
those unjustly imprisoned or sent to labor camps by the MVD's
special commissions and to rid the MVD of all repressive functions. His son says that some members of the Presidium were
in favor, but that Khrushchev was against. He then presented
a resolution suggesting that this was "premature" (see ibid.,

---

[1] Ibid., p. 257.
[2] Ibid.

p. 259). As we have seen previously, Beria's plan to convene a special congress at which all members of the presidium and the Central Committee should openly tell the general public what role they each had played during the repressions in the 1930s came to nothing.

In Georgia, a right-wing putsch had taken place led by Khrushchev's close confidant Semyon D. Ignatiev, with high-ranking party officials being arrested and put into jail on false pretexts. Thousands were arrested and forced to "admit" that Beria, the former leader of the Georgian Communist Party, was a "bourgeois nationalist." Beria annulled all decisions taken to that effect and reinstated the former government. Ignatiev was expelled from the Central Committee and even from the party. After Beria's arrest, Khrushchev rehabilitated the putschist Ignatiev and he was readmitted to the Central Committee.

Other initiatives could be mentioned, among them the abolition of the old passport laws forcing workers to stay at their places of work, or his attempts to reform the nationalities policy of the USSR and to dismiss those politicians who had been sent from Moscow to take up important posts in the capitals of the republics, even though they could not speak the local languages. The politicians deposed by Beria, among them Nikolai S. Patoli-chev, then became some of his fiercest adversaries and slandered him at the crucial July Plenum with special venom.

The long list of his activities shows how energetic he was and how determined to change the state apparatus in a direction more in keeping with the old constitution of 1936, and to guarantee the constitutional rights and freedoms of the ordinary people laid down in the Soviet constitution (Articles 118 to 133). After his fall, all these initiatives were annulled; the Party again became the leading force, or, to be more precise, the nomencla-ture ruling the Party organizations. The Party again became the leading force in regulating the economy. The other government bodies, the Council of Ministers, the official Soviet government, and the Supreme Soviet, the legislative organ of the USSR under the Soviet constitution, were again subordinated to the Commu-nist Party. Nominations for leading positions in these organs were made by the Presidium and confirmed by the Central Committee. The Central Committee was no longer controlled by the MVD, as was the case at the time of Beria's 112-day interregnum. The security services MVD and MGB were turned into the Soviet KGB, and Khrushchev's crony Ivan Serov, who was appointed its chief, no longer had the right to control the party leaders.

The violent removal of Beria was a violent removal of his reform initiatives and the restoration of the old status quo. The Soviet constitution remained a declaration of intentions and was by and large ignored by the top echelon of the Party. Khrushchev's admission that the people would decide because the Party was the same as the people, and that he was the Party, so he would decide, materialized. This led to a whole series of bad decisions and even outright blunders committed by the new First Secretary and led to a growing alienation between the ordinary party member and the leadership, and even more so between the ordinary Soviet citizens and the Communist Party and its leaders. The highly praised "collective leadership" after Stalin's death came to nothing and was substituted by Khrushchev's rule and that of his cronies, among them his own son-in-law, Alexei Adzhubei, who became his chief adviser on foreign policy issues.

Khrushchev had won the dominant influence in the Party after Beria's arrest. In September of 1953, he officially became First Secretary of the CPSU, and now he could start his own "reforms" designed to dismantle Soviet socialism and to restore capitalism in the Soviet Union.

Khrushchev's Capitalist Reforms and Their Outcome

After the arrest and execution of Beria, the main obstacle was removed for the new Soviet nomenclature to become the ruling class or at least the ruling elite in the Soviet Union. This removed the main stumbling block for dismantling the Soviet economic system that had come into being after the October Revolution in 1917. Now it could be transformed into a basically capitalist economy up to the mid-1960s.

The only opposition left that could conceivably throw a spanner into the works of that counterrevolutionary project was a handful of old Bolsheviks. These old "cranks" were Molotov, Malenkov and Kaganovich, who were still members of the Presidium of the CPSU after Beria's ouster. They kept issuing warnings that such an undertaking might lead to catastrophe, to a grave crisis in the USSR, and maybe also to its collapse in the long run. Four years after Beria's demise, they attempted to get rid of Khrushchev and replace him with former Defense Minister Bulganin. They hoped Bulganin could remedy the many blunders committed by First Secretary Khrushchev, especially in the sphere of agriculture.

But they failed, due to the concerted action of Marshal Zhukov and KGB chief Serov, who reinstalled Khrushchev as party leader when they organized an improvised CC Plenum in Moscow to reverse the decision taken by the Presidium. Molotov, Malenkov and Kaganovich had to go; they were later even expelled from the Communist Party and henceforth called an "Anti-Party Group" in Soviet historiography.

If we look at what the people around Khrushchev actually did after their illegal coup in June 1953, we can draw major conclusions as to why they were so eager to depose Beria. Tracing back their actions can lead to the conclusion that the putsch against Beria was a counterrevolutionary measure to remove not just a certain strong personality and his followers in the party hierarchy for one reason or another, but to pave the way for the introduction of a completely new social and economic system in the USSR.

It could lead to the conclusion that Khrushchev was the head of the Soviet counterrevolution, the successor of Trotsky and Bukharin who had failed to do just that in the 1920s and 1930s. This would provide us with the ultimate answer to the question why they arrested and murdered Beria in the first place.

Khrushchev disrupts the Soviet planning system

Politicians and other "great historic personalities" must always be judged by their actions and not by their many words and declarations of intention. What did the Khrushchevites, as the Albanian leader Enver Hoxha called Khrushchev's group in his memoirs, do as concerns the Soviet planning system, which had been a cornerstone of Soviet socialism under Lenin and Stalin and that had led to an unprecedented unknown economic upswing in the Soviet Union?

The five-year plan adopted by the 19th Party Congress in early October 1952, which constituted a binding law for all Soviet enterprises and managers of enterprises and combines, was being tampered with immediately after Beria's removal from power. Wolfgang Leonhard, a German observer, noted at the time:

> The decisions [to meddle with the current plan — author] led to a complete revision of the five-year plan for 1950–1955, which had been adopted when Stalin was still alive. The five-year plan provided for an increase in ready-to-wear clothing of 80 per cent from 1950. Now the increase was to be 240 per cent instead; with meat the increase no longer was to be 90 per cent but 230; with butter instead of 70 per cent, now 190; with textiles no longer 70 but now 180 per cent.[1]

Soon after Beria was removed, a whole avalanche of decrees were issued to revise the plan indices approved of by the 19th Party Congress, as New York Times correspondent Harry Schwartz noted:

> The original plan, for example, had called for 2.4 times as many sewing machines to be sold in 1955 as in 1950; the new plan set the target at 5.1 times. The original plan had predicted a doubling of radio and television sales; the new document called for 1955 sales of these items to be 4.4 times their 1950 level.[2]

The outcome: The program was not achieved. Schwartz again:

> The actual improvement in Soviet living standards in 1955 as compared with 1953 was well under what Malenkov, Khrushchev, and Mikoyan had explicitly promised.[3]

---

[1] Wolfgang Leonhard, *Kreml ohne Stalin*, Cologne and Berlin, 1963, pp. 74f.
[2] Harry Schwartz, *The Soviet Economy since Stalin*, Philadelphia and New York, 1965, p. 61.
[3] Ibid., p. 62.

The measures, showing a growing disrespect by the new Soviet leaders for the once "holy" Soviet five-year plan, led to a considerable loss of authority of the plan and to its subsequent failure. *Cui bono* — who benefits?, one may ask: Those who wanted to do without any central planning and to reintroduce a "free market economy" Western-style.

After the 20th Party Congress in 1956, when Khrushchev's people had won a solid majority of seats in the Central Committee, a completely different and totally unrealistic plan, the Sixth Five-Year Plan, was adopted, leading to its premature termination after only one and a half years. In 1959 this plan was replaced by an over-ambitious seven-year plan adopted at a special party congress which collapsed after only five years. For the whole year of 1958 no Five-Year Plan existed at all. Roy and Zhores A. Medvedev wrote in 1976:

> But it must be acknowledged that, from 1958 on, he was leading the nation to the brink of economic catastrophe and the unfortunate aftereffects of many of the projects and programs of 1958–64 are still being felt in the Soviet Union.[1]

Another event shows complete disrespect for socialist planning: In 1964, two factories of the textile industry were chosen and freed from any restrictions imposed by the central plan — a pilot scheme for the upcoming great economic reform of 1965 under Kosygin. The plant directors were allowed to set up their own production plan and were given powers they never enjoyed before, powers to act like Western managers, following the profit principle as the main criterion for social production.

Khrushchev decentralizes the Soviet planning system

To introduce parts of the American system, where the state has no role in the economy, Khrushchev reorganized the entire governmental system, starting with agriculture. Ministries based in Moscow were shut down, to be reopened in the provinces. The Ministry for Agriculture was closed; it reopened its branches in the countryside around large collective farms. The

---

[1] Roy and Zhores A. Medvedev, *Khrushchev. The Years in Power*, New York, 1976, preface, p. X.

agricultural ministries of other republics were shut down likewise and replaced by mere directors of large collective farms. Even professional agricultural academies were not spared and had to resettle in the provinces.

In the entire Soviet Union more than one hundred regional planning bodies were created, called "Sovnarkhozy," to decentralize, but in fact to sabotage, planning.

As from 1955, collective farms gained the right to draw up their own plans; they no longer had to abide by central planning indices, which still existed but were treated as mere recommendations. The Medvedev brothers' comment:

> Khrushchev wanted to do more than simply transplant the American system where the state had a mere advisory function. He therefore reorganized the entire government structure, including the agricultural ministries, the larger and middle-level agrarian institutes and colleges, and the experimental stations...So he ordered the Ministry of Agriculture of the Soviet Union to leave Moscow, move to a rural area, and set up a large model farm there, a kind of permanent agricultural exhibition of nationwide relevance.[1]

The entire personnel was transferred to the large Mikhailovskoe sovkhoz, costing the Soviet taxpayer the amount of 50 billion rubles, as Roy and Zhores A. Medvedev note. Respected agricultural academies were dying a slow death in the process, among them the Timiryazev Academy for Agricultural Questions.

This marked the end of central planning and the beginning of a free-market economy, Soviet-style.

Khrushchev's Virgin Land Program

Wolfgang Leonhard writes about Khrushchev's program to shift the emphasis of agricultural production to his project to develop vast areas of virgin land:

> The joint decision of the leadership of the Party and the state taken on March 28 to develop new estates in 1954 and 1955 meant that the largest part of the yearly Soviet

---

[1] Ibid., p. 111.

production of agricultural machines, among them 10,000 combine harvesters and 120,000 tractors, was to be used for the Virgin Land Program.[1]

The Virgin Land project quickly became a huge flop. Subordinated to Khrushchev's favorite pastime, agricultural production decreased continuously after 1958. This should surprise nobody: to develop new areas the size of France in the East, a huge amount of agricultural machinery had to be mobilized, machinery now missing for ordinary agricultural production. Farm laborers were also becoming hard to come by on those collective farms engaged in ordinary production, as they were urgently needed for the new project.

Khrushchev sells the Machine Tractor Stations to the farms

In 1958 Khrushchev had a new brainstorm: Why not sell the machine tractor stations (MTS) to the collective farms? Until then, the stations had been providing the kolkhozes with well-qualified agricultural specialists and modern machinery free of charge. Now the collective farms would have to buy the MTS, thus becoming proprietors of the machines. The specialists either had to join the farms or find different jobs in the cities. The farms, especially the smaller and less productive ones, could not afford to buy the machinery and had to take out loans to finance the purchase; this forced them to economize and to scale down agricultural production.

By the end of 1958, more than 80 percent of all farms had bought former MTS machinery, writes William Taubman, Khrushchev's biographer. Then he adds:

> The consequences were devastating. After paying for their new machinery, even better-off farms couldn't afford other needed investments. Meanwhile, they made less efficient use of their new equipment than the MTS had. MTS workers had been a kind of elite. Since those who transferred to the kolkhozes suffered a drop in status and income, many fled to the cities. The result,

---

[1] Wolfgang Leonhard, *Kreml ohne Stalin*, ibid., p.78.

according to Roy Medvedev, was that "farm production suffered irreparable damage."[1]

Even Molotov, who had always supported Khrushchev, especially against Beria, was displeased and is reported as saying that this measure was "anti-Marxist" and "destroying our socialist achievements."[2]

Here is a table showing the development of agricultural production in the 1950s and 1960s,[3] with 1958 as the benchmark.

Year	Crop Output
1958	100
1959	95
1960	100
1963	86

100 = total crop output in 1958, data for 1958–1962 recalculated to 1958 from *Narodnoye Khosyaistvo SSSR v 1962 godu*.

In 1963, the situation in Soviet agriculture became so critical that, for the first time in the history of the USSR, grain had to be imported from Canada, the US and Romania to safeguard food supplies. Schwartz sums it up this way:

> The actual result, as we know, was nearly catastrophic... In 1963 the government had procured only 44,800,000 metric tons of grain, more than 20 per cent less than the 1962 procurements, and more than one third below the 70–75,000,000 tons Khrushchev had called for. The results were swift and drastic: sharp limitations on bread sales were imposed in the Soviet Union and government buyers fanned out to the Western world to buy millions of tons of grain from the United States, Canada, and

---

[1] William Taubman, *Khrushchev. The Man and His Era*, ibid., p. 376.

[2] Ibid.

[3] *Narodnoye Khozyaistvo SSSR v 1962 godu*, p. 227, in: Harry Schwartz, *The Soviet Economy since Stalin*, ibid., p. 130.

other Western nations. The Khrushchev agricultural program had resulted in a fiasco.[1]

The agricultural crisis brought about by his policy was bound to lead to hunger, especially in the southern regions, giving rise to widespread revolts. To avert such a scenario the Soviet government decided to sell part of the Soviet gold reserves to the West as sufficient foreign currency reserves were not available:

> Calamity could be averted only by enormous purchases of grain and other foodstuffs from abroad, although this would be the first time that such extensive emergency measures had ever been required, either in tsarist or Soviet history...Ingots were shipped to the London gold market, the first consignment a total of 500 tons.[2]

Khrushchev reintroduces foreign debt

Whereas the Soviet Union under Lenin and Stalin had annulled all foreign debt soon after the October Revolution and attached great importance to remaining debt-free to guarantee the economic and political independence of the country from imperialism, the Khrushchev regime soon started taking out large loans in the West to finance industry, for example its new chemical industry. Schwartz:

> [Khrushchev], declaring his country had a "big appetite" for Western capital, suggested that the Soviet Union would be interested in borrowing as much as a billion pounds, almost three billion dollars...The debate waxed even hotter in the early fall of 1964 when the British government guaranteed a 15-year credit worth $ 67,000,000 to permit the Soviet Union to buy equipment for a polyester fiber plant. About the same time Japan granted the Soviet Union an eight-year credit to finance the purchase of a $10,000,000 fertilizer plant. Later France promised seven-year-credits totaling several hundred million dollars.[3]

Khrushchev's economic policy allowing foreign debt was a harbinger of what was to happen during the Brezhnev and

---

[1] H. Schwartz, ibid., p. 169.
[2] Roy and Zhores A. Medvedev, *Khrushchev. The Years in Power*, ibid., p. 160.
[3] Ibid., pp. 200f.

Gorbachev years, but even more so in the era of Boris Yeltsin, when Russia became a semi-colony of the United States.

Khrushchev splits the Party

To introduce something like a two-party system similar to that in the United States, Khrushchev issued a decree to split all Party organizations into two sections: one for industrial and another for agricultural affairs. All Soviet republics were obliged to follow the Moscow example: a Central Committee for Industry and one for Agriculture was created dividing the entire party structure into two independent parts. Roy and Zhores A. Medvedev's comment on the measure:

> Something remotely like a two-party system had emerged, still unified by a common ideology and platform, but with all the potential problems of such a system.[1]

After Khrushchev's fall in October 1964, when he was deposed by his own followers who had assisted his rise to power in the early 1950s and supported his putsch against Beria, the measure was reversed and the old party structure reestablished. Khrushchev's Party reform was one of the main reasons for his removal, but not the only one.

Khrushchev appeases the West and starts reducing the Soviet military

Of course those credits were not given for nothing. As is standard practice at the IMF, for example, credits of that size are always linked to political concessions, and Khrushchev and his group who came to power after the Beria affair must have known that.

Already in his first years in power, he cut down the Soviet military which, as we have seen, brought him to power in the first place. Zhukov, the man who twice acted on his behalf to keep him in office, was dismissed by the new First Secretary in the autumn of 1957 while on a visit to the Balkans. Khrushchev now advanced his idea that all it takes to defend a country the size of the Soviet Union is a couple of missiles. The Soviet army

---

[1] Ibid., p. 155.

was downgraded. Even in the first years of his term more than a million Soviet soldiers were sent home. Taubman:

> Between 1955 and 1957 the USSR unilaterally reduced Soviet troop strength by more than 2 million men. In January 1958, another 300,000 were cut, and in January 1960 Khrushchev announced a further reduction of 1.2 million troops, including 250,000 officers. What particularly galled the military was that, with no preparations made for housing and employing thousands of former officers, many were in effect dumped in the street. Before long, grumbling could be heard in almost all branches of the armed services. In the spring of 1962, a naval captain visiting the young diplomat Arkady Shevchenko described how fellow officers "had wept as they watched nearly completed cruisers and destroyers at the docks in Leningrad being cut up for scrap on Khrushchev's orders."[1]

Khrushchev's unilateral disarmament decision came at a time when the Cold War had only just started and no end was in sight, and later further steps in the same direction were taken to appease the Americans.

In 1958, the US senator and Democratic presidential hopeful Hubert Humphrey spent some time in Moscow, also visiting Khrushchev in the Kremlin. After a conversation lasting eight hours, he said:

> This is a man who is very much up our line...Just the sort of man with whom a man like Ike [President Dwight D. Eisenhower] could do business.[2]

Five years earlier, when making his speech against Beria at the July Plenum, Khrushchev had still posed as a hardliner, telling the delegates:

> Now that we have liberated ourselves from this dirty swine and now that we have eliminated Beria, the enemy, we shall even more securely march forward towards new victories.[3]

---

[1] William Taubman, *Khrushchev. The Man and his Era*, ibid., pp. 379F, citing Arkady P. Shevchenko, *Breaking with Moscow*, New York, 1985, p. 93.

[2] Ibid., p. 408.

[3] Viktor Knoll and Lothar Kölm, *Der Fall Berija*, ibid., p. 71.

So these were some of Khrushchev's "reforms," which could also be called steps in the direction of restoring capitalism in the Soviet Union. The difference between them and Lavrenti Beria's own reforms (here the word needn't be put in quotation marks) is that Beria intended to restore the Soviet constitution of 1936; Khrushchev wanted to restore capitalism.

The Results of Eleven Years of Khrushchevism: Chronic Crises and Social Unrest

The Soviet Union under Stalin strictly adhered to solid Marxist principles which needed to be observed for the construction of socialism. What happens if production plans, for example, do not follow these principles and the "laws" for building socialism? Stalin put it in a nutshell in the early 1950s, in one of his conversations with leading Soviet economists:

> All existing laws react if one tries to break or ignore them. Someone who does this is always punished in the aftermath.[1]

If economic planning in socialism does not observe the law of a planned and proportional development of the national economy, if the planners are of the opinion that this law can be ignored and not be taken into account, and they draw up a five-year plan that is completely unrealistic and arbitrary, the law will make itself felt. One is punished and has to bear the unpleasant results. What kind of results? Economic crises, supply shortages, disproportions in the economy, economic stagnation, hidden unemployment, and social unrest in the aftermath.

Stalin told his economists, who were working on a textbook on Political Economy:

> So we need a planned economy. It is not our wish; it is inevitable or everything will collapse.[2]

And this would happen in the Soviet Union, first under Khrushchev and later under Gorbachev. But before the collapse of the Soviet Union became a reality in 1991, the first crises

---

[1] *Conversations with Stalin on Questions of Political Economy*, Working Paper No. 33, document 1, from Russian Archives, translated into English by Ethan Pollock, at: http://wilsoncenter.org/sites/default/filesACFBO7.pdf,
[2] Ibid.

started to emerge here and there which then became chronic in the later stages of Khrushchev's term in office and also under the Brezhnev regime.

Soon after the introduction of the Khrushchev "reforms," the first harbingers of a grave economic and social crisis appeared on the horizon: rising prices and chronic inflation; supply short-ages as regards foodstuffs and other consumer goods; rigid increases of factory output norms and a growing dissatisfaction among the Soviet population, especially in southern Russia.

In 1962, the first strikes occurred in the Northern Caucasus in the city of Novocherkassk, and they soon spread to other cities, among them Kiev and even Moscow. Khrushchev's biog-rapher, William Taubman, writes:

> On May 17, 1962, the Presidium approved a draft govern-ment decree scheduled to take effect on June 2, raising retail prices by as much as 35 percent for meat and poultry products and by up to 25 percent for butter and milk...To make matters worse, the price rise followed a move to raise factory output norms by requiring more work for the same pay or less pay for the same work...But Khrushchev insisted on taking full responsibility.[1]

The price hikes came into effect on June 1. Immediately after-wards leaflets protesting them were distributed around the country and calls for strikes sounded in big cities like Moscow, Kiev, Donetsk and Chelyabinsk. Hardest hit, however, was the city of Novocherkassk. Taubman:

> The worst outbreak occurred at the huge Budenny Electric Locomotive Factory twelve miles outside the northern Caucasus city of Novocherkassk. As a result of work-norm increases, take-home pay there had fallen by as much as 30 percent. Workers had also complained about poor working conditions (two hundred had fallen sick in one shop), the high cost of housing, and shortages and high prices at the market in town.[2]

On one of the locomotives was written with chalk: "Cut up Khrushchev for meat!" (see ibid., p. 520). Taubman:

---

[1] William Taubman, *Khrushchev. The Man and his Era*, ibid., p. 519.
[2] Ibid.

[E]yewitnesses recalled that pictures of Khrushchev were ripped down, thrown in a heap, and then burned. In the middle of the afternoon the captured train was briefly liberated by KGB and local police, only to be retaken by the angry crowd. Party officials trying to read the Central Committee's defense of the price rise were drowned out. "We've read it ourselves," someone shouted. "We're literate, you know. Tell us instead how we're supposed to live with pay going down and prices going up!"

About two hundred police arrived at the factory between 6:00 and 7:00 P.M. but were soon forced to flee. The same fate awaited soldiers who drove up in five cars and three armored personnel carriers. According to the KGB, several who tried to restore "law and order" were beaten by demonstrators. Strike meetings continued through the night at the plant, workings arriving the next morning joined in, and at about 8:00 A.M. on June 2, the massive crowd headed for the city.[1]

One day later, the workers of the plant, together with their wives and children, marched into the city carrying red flags and portraits of Marx and Lenin. Workers from other plants joined them on their way. The demonstration was entirely peaceful. But when they tried to cross the bridge over the Tuzlov River, they were confronted with tanks blocking the bridge. So they waded through the water, tried to climb over the tanks, or bypassed them. The soldiers made no attempt to stop them. At the Lenin Square the main Party headquarters was occupied, and speeches were made on the balcony. Then the first warning shots were fired; after that the soldiers fired directly into the crowd. Twenty-three people, mostly young men, were killed, 87 wounded; three more died later. Of the dead, two were women and one was a schoolboy (see Taubman, ibid., p. 521). The official Soviet media ignored the event to forestall further unrest. In the official history of the Communist Party of the Soviet Union (Moscow, 1971), no mention is made of the events.

---

[1] Ibid.

Later Khrushchev's Prosecutor General, Roman Rudenko, the man he had arbitrarily and illegally appointed for the Beria trial in December 1953, condemned seven strike leaders to death.

The events provide ample evidence to the fact that Khrushchev and his cronies had no scruples about shedding the blood of the Russian working class if they presented a serious challenge, and they did not have any scruples either when it came to murdering senior Soviet politicians to get to power, among them Stalin. This, Khrushchev and his crony Mikoyan proudly admitted in open public, shedding a bit of light on their "Communist" morality as well.[1]

Events similar to those in Novocherkassk had also occurred some years earlier in April, 1956, in Georgia, Stalin's home country, where a crowd of 60,000 gathered in Tbilisi to commemorate Stalin's death. Taubman:

> On the third anniversary of his death Georgians gathered in the streets of Tbilisi and several other cities. What began as a peaceful tribute to Stalin turned into four days of violent protests against Khrushchev's secret speech. More than 60,000 people carried flowers to the Stalin monument in Tbilisi, while hundreds of others with portraits of Stalin careered around the city in trucks and commandeered buses, trams, and trolleys. "Glory to the Great Stalin!" "Down with Khrushchev!"...When they marched on the radio station, troops and tanks moved in. In two clashes alone, one of them at the Stalin monument, 15 were killed and 54 were wounded; five of them died subsequently. In the end at least 20 demonstrators were killed, 60 wounded and many arrested and imprisoned.[2]

In October 1964, Khrushchev was deposed by his former friends in a silent coup and henceforth called an "unperson." He was no longer mentioned in the media. Later he wrote his

---

[1] The use of poison seems to be accepted; stories casting blame vary. Interview with Poltoranin. *Russia Insider*, May 17 2018. https://russia-insider.com/en/inessa-s, also Smithsonianmag.com. October 10, 2017, https://www.smithsonianmag.com/history/true-story-death-stalin-180965119/; and "New Study Supports Idea Stalin Was Poisoned," The New York Times, https://www.nytimes.com/2003/03/05/world/new-study-supports-idea-stalin-was-poisoned.html.

[2] Ibid., pp. 286f.

memoirs, which he then smuggled out of the country so that they could be published by his American publisher. Some members of the Central Committee wanted to put him on trial, but he was treated leniently by his successors, given a dacha and sent into early retirement, dying a peaceful death in 1971.

Leonid Brezhnev, one of Khrushchev's cronies, was given the top job in the Soviet hierarchy. To remind the reader: Brezhnev belonged to the group of young officers Zhukov had brought with him to arrest Beria on June 26 at the meeting of the Presidium, if we follow the official version. Brezhnev stood guard to make sure that the coup against Beria was not disturbed by the Kremlin guards.

Verification of the Working Hypothesis

Do we have evidence enough to call Nikita Khrushchev a counterrevolutionary and an enemy of socialism? I think we have. Let's sum up some of the evidence briefly, bearing in mind the need to judge politicians and statesmen according to their deeds and not according to their many words. We can forget about the fact that Khrushchev on numerous occasions called himself a Communist.

1. Khrushchev dismantled the socialist planning system to introduce the beginnings of a "free market economy." Do committed Communists do such a thing?

2. Khrushchev split the Communist Party. Do Communists do such a thing or do they attach importance on having a unified and strong Marxist party?

3. Khrushchev is responsible for at least two massacres, one in 1956 in Georgia and another in 1962, when he gave orders to shoot at workers who were peacefully demonstrating and protesting, as his biographer Taubman told us in great detail.

4. Khrushchev even dismantled the Soviet army to appease the United States and he demobilized more than a million soldiers without getting anything in return from the imperialists. Do real Communists do such a thing or do they stand up to imperialism?

I could enumerate lots of additional facts testifying that Khrushchev was not a Communist but a covert Social Democrat, an opportunist who betrayed not just socialism but also his mother country, and not just during his eleven-year term in office but even before that, under Stalin, especially in the Ukraine where he was head of the Ukrainian Communist Party for ten years.

This man came into power by a violent coup in June of 1953, thus treating the Soviet constitution of 1936 with contempt as this constitution does not allow such a thing. So we can also call him an enemy of the Soviet constitution. The coup made a lot of sense: By enabling Khrushchev and his group to get the top positions in the country, the ensuing "reforms" which I have just mentioned could be launched to gradually sabotage and dismantle Soviet socialism and to replace it with a Russian chauvinist type of capitalism.

When he was on his deathbed in 1971, this "Communist" admitted that he had only contempt for socialism. When he had a heart attack in late 1970, he was placed not in the heart patients' ward but in the neurological section, where he felt better soon and started joking to the nurse treating him.

> It was there, shortly after he began to feel better, that the doctor in charge of his treatment, Praskovia Moshentseva, found him reading Pravda. When she hesitated to interrupt him, he laughingly insisted he was just reading about socialism, which he described as "only water."

> She tried to ignore that and concentrate on his intravenous tubes, but he told her a story about a party lecturer who consumed three glasses of water while rambling on endlessly to an indifferent audience of collective farmers. When the lecturer asked for questions, there were none until a short peasant in the back row stood up. "Respected lecturer," he said, "here you go and talk about socialism for three hours, you drink three glasses of water, and not once do you take a leak. How can that be?"

Dr. Moshentseva was mortified, but her patient shook with laughter. "Now you know what socialism is," he said. "It's water."[1]

So we can safely say that Khrushchev was an enemy of socialism who had wormed his way into the Communist Party of the Soviet Union as early as the 1920s, after he had publicly "regretted" having belonged to a Trotskyite group, with the aim to reach the top position one day to enable him to dismantle the tried and tested socialist system and to also split the world communist movement.

As class struggle continues, during the period of building socialism, enemies of socialism are systematically placed in leading positions by a hidden counterrevolutionary movement supported by the imperialist environment and their secret services that operate clandestinely in a socialist country with especial fervor to bring down the hated system. These "Communists," often recruited by these services, then try to "prove" that they are hard-line "Communists," sworn "Marxists-Leninists," to win esteem and to reach the top. They often denounce honest Communists and Marxists and call them "agents of imperialism," "enemies of the people," or "anti-party elements," as did Khrushchev and his circle of followers.

They start witch-hunts to get rid of sincere Communists and Marxists, or by outright purges (on behalf of Communism, of course). If a Communist Party is ideologically weak and if Marxism has not taken firm roots there, these covert actors can become successful. Khrushchev became successful, very successful, even though he was removed in the end from the top position, due to his many blunders; his maneuvers did not serve the Soviet counterrevolution well but created growing unrest in the country, as we have seen. Reason enough to replace him with other so-called Communists, better suited to do the same job. After Khrushchev's "reforms," Kosygin's "reforms" were initiated in the mid-sixties.

---

[1] Ibid., p. 640.

Conclusion

From my analysis the following conclusion can be drawn:

The violent and unconstitutional removal of Lavrenti P. Beria from office as Soviet Interior Minister and Deputy Prime Minister of the USSR, the number two in the hierarchy, was not just any kind of power struggle or rivalry between two adversaries. It was a counterrevolutionary coup to bring to power a group of politicians whose intention it was to dismantle the Soviet socialist system and, in the long run, to restore capitalism in the nation.

Khrushchev was one of the key figures, maybe the chief organizer of the coup, backed by a leading group of Soviet military men, among them Georgi Zhukov and Kirill Moskalenko. For his "excellent organizing job" in getting rid of Stalin and Beria, as well as for his pro-capitalist views, Khrushchev was given the top job in the party hierarchy in September 1953.

EPILOGUE

Myths and legends are very tough and persistent. Often they are repeated for centuries, even for millennia, without being questioned. Hitler's propaganda chief Joseph Goebbels wrote that "Churchill...holds to his lies, and in fact repeats them until he himself believes them. That is an old English trick. Mr. Churchill does not need to perfect it, as it is one of the familiar tactics of British politics, known to the entire world."[1]

A lie that is repeated over and over again will, in the end, be considered to be a truth. We only need to think of the many stories of so-called saints spread by the churches for centuries on end to manipulate people's minds in the interest of preserving their power, to captivate the minds and hearts of ordinary people and to be able to control as many of them as possible and also their daily lives. People are encouraged to believe and worship instead of thinking clearly and independently. Those who do think for themselves are seen as a potential threat.

The legend of Beria the sadist, the monster, the rapist, the GPU man who in cold blood sent thousands and thousands

---

[1] Joseph Goebbels. "Aus Churchills Lügenfabrik" (Churchill's Lie Factory), *Die Zeit ohne Beispiel* (Munich: Zentralverlag der NSDAP., 1941), pp. 364-369. https://research.calvin.edu/german-propaganda-archive/goeb29.htm

of innocent people into the Gulag and into prisons, is still not being challenged after so many decades have elapsed since he died. The same can be said of Joseph Stalin.

Where is the first honest historian, the first history professor in a Western country, who is not wearing anti-Communist blinkers, who would think for one moment and at least add some question marks to those sensational stories spread by the Russian counterrevolution and their many helpers in the Western media? Who will put this one key question to himself and ask, Who benefited most from all these stories and who still does? Cui bono? Who, in general, benefits from historical myths? The answer: Those who came to power illegally and violently.

British Communist Bill Bland once said in a lecture on the topic of "Stalinism":

> Perhaps the nearest figure to Stalin in British history is Richard the Third, whom everybody "knows" — and I put the word "knows" in quotation marks — from their school history books and Shakespeare to have been a cruel, deformed monster who murdered the little princess in the Tower.

> It's only been comparatively recently that serious historians have begun to realize that the commonly accepted portrait of Richard was drawn up by his Tudor successors who had seized the throne from him and killed him.

> Naturally, they then proceeded to rewrite the chronicles to justify their usurpation of the throne — even altering his portraits to present him as physically deformed, as a physical as well as a moral monster. In other words, the picture of Richard which has become generally accepted today was the result not of historical truth but of propaganda by his political opponents. It is therefore legitimate to ask: Is the picture of Stalin presented to us by so-called "Kremlinologists" historical fact or mere propaganda?[1]

This can also be said about Beria, one of Stalin's closest collaborators all through his years in power. Those who captured the "throne" in June of 1953 in the Kremlin, the Khrushchev people,

---

[1] William B. Bland, *Stalinism*, an address to the Sarat Academy in London, April 30, 1999, at: http://espressostalinist.com/2011/09/16/bill-bland-on-stalinism/

the successors of the old Soviet Trotskyite opposition, rewrote history soon after Beria's removal, as we have already seen.

The Great Soviet Encyclopedia was the first victim. The Soviet chronicles were rewritten. In the history of the Communist Party of the Soviet Union (first published in Moscow in 1971), we read:

> The Presidium of the Central Committee of the Party exposed these hostile plans. In July 1953, the Plenum of the CC unanimously approved of resolute measures to liquidate Beria's criminal activity. It was revealed that this political adventurer had grossly violated legality over a long period of time, that he had fabricated accusations against honest Party and state officials and had them killed. Beria and his accomplices were taken before court and received the deserved punishment.[1]

The "deserved punishment" was a death sentence, but other people also received this "deserved punishment," among them the former Soviet ambassador to Berlin, Dekanozov, who is not mentioned by the "History." As we have seen, Beria was not the only one to meet Khrushchev's wrath.

The same "History" ignores Khrushchev's massacres in Georgia and Novocherkassk and also his role as party chief in the Ukraine, where he was deeply involved in Yezhov's mass murders in 1937 and 1938 as a member of one of the infamous "Troikas" — courts of three people passing verdicts on party members after having used lists of people, said to be "enemies" and who were executed after a ten-minute hearing with no recourse to an appeal. The "History" was used as a standard textbook to teach millions of young Communists in the post-Stalin Soviet Union the "truth" about the Soviet past, and I myself as a young Communist bought it in a German bookshop, read it and believed every word.

I can only think of one historian who has meanwhile done excellent work in this field and who has indeed questioned the long-established Beria legend: Professor Grover C. Furr. But such people are a rare exception to the rule, and they are vilified, even by — or especially by — colleagues working in the same

---

[1] Boris N. Ponomarjow, et al, *History of the Communist Party of the Soviet Union,* Berlin, 1973, p. 693.

field of research. Will they find a publisher who is independent thinking and courageous enough to print their alternative point of view? And what is even more disturbing: How can those who consider themselves to be rational, educated people accept at face value the many stories spread about Lavrenti P. Beria and his legacy. And again: Roughly the same can be said about his closest collaborator: J. Stalin.

It is time to do some objective historic research, and time to base judgments on hard, historical facts.

APPENDIX

1/ Beria put an end to illegal mass arrests and executions, 1939

In the Ukraine, where Khrushchev is still head of the Ukrainian Communist Party, the repressions continue however until 1940. Beria was appointed new head of the NKVD (Ministry of the Interior, including the Secret Service) in 1939 at Stalin's behest. Nicolai Yezhov, his predecessor, who was chiefly responsible for the mass murders, was executed in 1941. In his memoirs, Khrushchev called Yezhov an "honest Communist."

Arrests in the USSR between 1935 and 1940

1935	1936	1937	1938	1939	1940
114,456	88,873	918,671	629,695	41,627	127,313

Executed

| 1,229 | 1,118 | 353,074 | 328,618 | 2,601 | 1,863 |

Sources: at http://msuweb.montclair.edu/~furrg/research/ezhovin~
terrogs.html. (Yezhov's confessions); numbers from: Pospelov
report, at: http://alexanderyakovlev.org/almanah/inside/
almanah~doc/55752, see Grover Furr, *Khrushchev Lied*, Kettering/
Ohio, July 2011, p. 328.

2/ Zhukov, the thief

Soviet Marshal and "Hero of the Soviet Union," Georgi K.
Zhukov, who brought Khrushchev to power in a coup on June
26, 1953, had been found guilty of having kept large amounts of
looted German treasure for himself. Stalin then demoted Zkukov.
In this Secret Speech Khrushchev said: "After the war Stalin
began to tell all kinds of nonsense about Zhukov..." Beria and
his security chief (head of the Soviet MGB), Viktor Abakumov,
wanted to arrest Zhukov, but failed to do so (excerpt):

Top Secret

THE COUNCIL OF MINISTERS OF THE USSR:

To comrade STALIN J. V.

...During the night of 8–9 January of this year, a secret
search was conducted of Zhukov's dacha, which is situ~
ated in the village of Rublevo near Moscow.

As a result of this search, it was disclosed that two rooms
of the dacha had been converted into storerooms in
which a huge quantity of goods and valuables of various
kinds are stored.

For example:

Woolen fabrics, silk, brocade, velvet, and other materials
— in all, more than 4,000 meters; furs, sable, monkey,
fox, sealskin, Astrakhan (fine wool), a total of 323 hides;
Kidskin of the best quality — 35 skins; valuable carpets
and Gobelin rugs of very large size from the Potsdam and
other palaces and homes of Germany — 44 pieces in all,
some of which are laid or hung in various rooms, and the
rest in the storeroom.

Especially worthy of note is a carpet of great size placed in one of the rooms of the dacha; valuable paintings of classical landscapes of very large sizes in artistic frames — 55 units in all, hung in various rooms of the dacha and a part of which remain in the storeroom.

Very expensive table and tea services (porcelain with artistic decoration, crystal) — 7 large chests; accordions with rich artistic decoration — 8 units; unique hunting rifles by the firm Gotland — Gotland and others — 20 units in all.

This property is kept in 51 trunks and suitcases, and also lies in heaps.

Besides that in all the rooms of the dacha, on the windows, staircase, tables and bedside tables are placed around great quantities of bronze and porcelain vases and statuettes of artistic work, and also all kinds of trinkets and knick-knacks of foreign origin.

I draw attention to the declaration by the workers who carried out the search that Zhukov's dacha is in essence an antique store or museum, with various valuable works of art hanging all around the interior...

There are so many valuable paintings that they could never be suitable for an apartment but should be transferred to the State fund and housed in a museum.

More than twenty large carpets cover the floor of almost all the rooms.

All the objects, beginning with the furniture, carpets, vessels, decorations, up to the curtains on the windows, are foreign, mainly German. There is literally not a single thing of Soviet origin in the dacha...

There is not a single Soviet book in the dacha, but on the other hand on the bookshelves stands a large quantity of books in beautiful bindings with gold embossing, all without exception in the German language.

When you go into the house, it is hard to imagine that one is not in Germany but near Moscow...

Accompanying this letter, please find photographs of some of the valuables, cloth and items we discovered in Zhukov's apartment and dacha.

ABAKUMOV *

January 10, 1948

*Viktor Abakumov, former chief of the MGB (Soviet State Security), arrested in 1951 on false charges, was sentenced to death by a military tribunal in 1954 after Khrushchev's rise to power. Beria and Abakumov wanted to arrest Zhukov and put him on trial after they had discovered the war booty in his dacha.

Source: *Voennie Arkhivy Rossii*,1993, pp. 189–191, at: http://chss.mont-clair.edu/english/furr/research/zhukovtheft4648_var93.pdf, see: Grover Furr, *Khrushchev Lied*, ibid., pp. 363ff.

3/ Zhukov's motive to arrest Beria

In his memoirs Soviet Marshal Georgi K. Zhukov tells us why he wanted to remove his arch-enemy Beria and how the operation was planned. He does not mention the war booty he had hidden in his dacha. His version of the events:

A risky operation.

Bulganin, who was Defense Minister at the time (1953-author), asked me to see him and take a seat. He was so agitated that he forgot to greet me. Only later he took my hand without a word of apology.

We didn't say a word. Then Bulganin said to me: "We are now driving to the Kremlin — an urgent matter!" We entered the room where the sessions of the Presidium of the CC of the Party usually take place. There I learned that a meeting of the Council of Ministers had been arranged. The ministers were all there. Beria was to give the report. I turned round. Malenkov, Molotov, Mikoyan, and the other members of the Presidium were present, but Beria was still missing.

Malenkov was the first to speak. He said that Beria wanted to seize power, and that I and my comrades should arrest him. Then it was Khrushchev's turn. Mikoyan only repeated that Beria constituted a danger and wanted to seize power.

"Can you handle this risky operation?" "Yes," was my answer. They knew that Beria and I had been enemies for years, that I even hated him. Even under Stalin I had words with him. I would only like to mention that Beria and Abakumov at one time wanted to arrest me. They had already obtained the keys to my dacha. When I returned from an official trip once, I noticed that my personal archive — diaries, notes, and photo albums — had disappeared. In spite of an intensive search I could not find them. Only much later, after three or four years, I got hold of them again. Malinovsky gave me a call at the time: "Georgi Konstantinovich, we have found two albums in the MVD's archive with photos where you can be seen together with Americans, Frenchmen, and other prominent persons. Do you want to have them?"

These albums which I had kept in my dacha together with my personal archive and which I was missing showed me that Beria and Abakumov had a finger in the pie. The whole arrangement of the photos had been altered to discredit me in the eyes of Stalin. By the way: Stalin once bluntly told me that I should be arrested. Beria tried to denounce me to Stalin, but he told him: "I cannot believe that this intrepid field marshal and patriot is a traitor. Stop slandering him!" So you will understand that after all what happened I had good reason to arrest Beria.

Malenkov described how the operation was to be staged: The session of the Council of Ministers is canceled, instead we convene a meeting of the Presidium. I was told to wait in a side room together with Moskalenko, Nedelin, Batisky, and Moskalenko's aide. I was given a warning that Beria was strong and a knew some judo. "We shall succeed, we are no weaklings!"

So we were waiting in the side room, and we had mean-while been waiting for an hour. I got nervous. Did anything unexpected happen in the committee room without our knowledge? Did Beria, this cunning intriguer and Stalin confidant, manage to outwit the others?

Around one o'clock a bell rang once, then twice. I stood up first...We entered the room. Beria was sitting at the table in the center. My generals went round the table as if they wanted to sit at the wall. I positioned myself behind Beria and said: "Stand up! You're under arrest!"

Before he could stand up, I tore his arms backwards and pushed him upwards. He was white as chalk and did not move. We led him through the side room and into another room with an emergency exit. There we searched him.

Oh, before I forget: When I grabbed Beria, I also checked if he was carrying a weapon. We only had one pistol with us. Later we got hold of a second one. We didn't know why we were ordered to the Kremlin, so we didn't take our weapons with us. Beria didn't have a weapon either. When he stood up, I gave his briefcase filled with lots of documents a push making it slide over the long and polished table.

We guarded him until 10 PM in the room I mentioned. After that, we took him out of the Kremlin. We pushed him on to the back seat of a ZIZ car (official government car — author) and covered him with a carpet. The Kremlin guard, who was subordinate to him, did not become suspicious and let us pass.

Moskalenko was driving. Beria was taken to the main police station, or to be more precise, to the prison of the Moscow military district. There he remained during the interrogations and also during the trial. There he was executed, too.

Source: Georgi K. Zhukov, *Reminiscences and Reflections*, 10th edition, Moscow, 1990, from: Vladimir F. Nekrassow, ed., *Berija-Henker in Stalins Diensten*, Augsburg, 1997, pp. 342ff.

4/ Excerpts from Khrushchev's anti-Beria speech at the July Plenum of the Central Committee of the Soviet Communist Party (July 2, 1953)

We've known Beria for many years. I've known him for twenty years. I knew him from the meetings of the Central Committee, and had to deal with him directly at work. I'd like to voice my opinion and my views about this type.

When Stalin was still alive, before we had a chance to form an opinion about his behavior and before we took the road of resolute action, we could see that Beria was a big intriguer. This is a devious person and a skilled careerist. With his dirty paws he had tightly embraced Stalin's soul, and he knew how to impose his opinion on him. He found ways and means to arouse skepticism as to one or the other question, he found ways and means to show someone in a bad light. At any time, he succeeded in setting Stalin against one or the other Party or state official. Impudence and impertinence — these are the most important qualities of Beria...

Beria tried to use the MVD for his dictatorship and to place the MVD above the Party...Without any doubt whatsoever it was his intention to undermine the friendship of the peoples, to stir up and to activate the bourgeois-nationalist elements...When we discussed the German question he clearly acted as a provocateur and agent of imperialism...

Source: Viktor Knoll und Lothar Kölm, eds., *Der Fall Berija. Protokoll einer Abrechnung,* verbatim shorthand minutes of the speeches held at the CC Plenum in July 1953, Berlin, 1999, pp. 47ff.

5/ On Khrushchev's past

Document 1: From his speech to the 14th Ukrainian Party Congress, 1938

Our cause is a holy cause. And he whose hand trembles, who stops half-way, whose knees shake before annihilating ten, a hundred enemies, exposes the Revolution to danger.

It is necessary to fight the enemies without mercy. Let us erase from the surface of the earth everybody who plans to attack the workers and peasants. We warn that for every drop of honest workers' blood we will shed a bucketful of the enemy's black blood.

Source: *Bolshevik Ukrainy*, No. 7, 1938, p. 11, from: Lazar Pistrak, *Khrushchev's Rise to Power*, New York, 1961, p. 153.

Document 2: Khrushchev had thousands of innocent people killed in 1936–38

N. S. Khrushchev, working as First Secretary of the MC (Moscow Committee) and the MCC (Moscow City Committee) of the ACP, b (Soviet Communist Party, Bolsheviks) in 1936–1937, and from 1937 as First Secretary of the CC of the C P(b)U (Communist Party of the Ukraine, Bolsheviks), personally gave his assent to the arrests of a significant number of Party and Soviet workers.

In the archive of the KGB there are documentary materials that attest to Khrushchev's participation in carrying out massive repressions in Moscow, Moscow district, and in the Ukraine in the prewar years. In particular, he personally sent documents with proposals for the arrests of leading workers of the Moscow Soviet and Moscow Oblast Committee of the Party to the NKVD. In all, during 1936–1937, 55,741 persons were repressed by the organs of the Moscow and Moscow district NKVD. From January 1938 Khrushchev headed the Party organization of the Ukraine. In 1938, 106,119 persons were arrested in the Ukraine. Repressions did not stop during the following years. In 1939 about 12,000 persons were arrested, and in 1940 — about 50,000 persons. In all, during the years 1938–1940 167,565 persons were arrested in the Ukraine.

The NKVD explained the increase in repressions in 1938 in the Ukraine in that, in connection with the arrival of Khrushchev, counter-revolutionary activity of the Right-Trotskyite underground grew especially quickly. Khrushchev personally sanctioned the repression of several hundred persons who were suspected of organizing terrorist acts (assassination attempts) against himself.

In the summer of 1938, with Khrushchev's consent, a large group of leading Party, Soviet, and economic workers were arrested, among them the vice-chairman of the Council of People's Commissars of the Ukrainian SSR, government ministers, assistant ministers, secretaries of district committees of the Party. All were sentenced to execution or to long terms of imprisonment. According to lists sent by the NKVD of the USSR to the Politburo, for 1938 alone permission was given for the repression of 2,140 persons of the republican Party and Soviet cadres.

Source: Excerpt from *Istochnik* No. 1, 1995, pp. 126F, *Rehabilitatsia. Kak eto bylo*, Moscow, 2004, pp. 146, 147, from: Grover Furr, *Khrushchev Lied*, ibid., pp. 255f.

6/ Khrushchev Mismanaging the Soviet Economy: Unfinished Projects in the USSR, 1958–1962

At End of Year	Capital Invested in Unfinished projects (billion rubles)	This Capital as % of year's total investment
1958	17.5	73
1959	19.0	90
1960	21.4	69
1961	24.8	76
1962	26.1	75

Source: *Narodnoye Khozyaistvo SSSR v 1962 godu*, p. 438, from: Harry Schwartz, *The Soviet Economy Since Stalin*, ibid., p. 136.

BIBLIOGRAPHY

Alliluyea, Svetlana, *Twenty Letters to a Friend: A Memoir* (Harper Perennial, 2016)

Beria, L., *Zur Geschichte der bolschewistischen Organisationen in Transkaukasien* (Verlag für fremdsprachige Literatur, 1940, in German)

_____*The Victory of the National Policy of Lenin and Stalin*, in: *The Selected Works of Lavrentiy Beria* (Prism Key Press, 2011)

_____*Diary* (Russia Today, April 2011)

Beria, Sergo, *Beria. My Father. Inside Stalin's Kremlin* (Duckworth, 2001)

Bland, William B., *About Stalinism*, at: http://espressostalinist. com/2011/16/bill-bland-on-stalinism

Furr, Grover, *Khrushchev Lied* (Erythros Press and Media, LLC, July 2011)

Keesing's Contemporary Archives, 1952–1954 (Bristol)

Knight, Amy, *Beria-Stalin's First Lieutenant* (Princeton University Press, 1993)

Knoll, Viktor and Kölm, Lothar, *Der Fall Berija*(Aufbau Taschenbuch Verlag, 1999, in German)

Leonhard, Wolfgang, *Kreml ohne Stalin* (Kiepenheuer & Witsch, 1963, in German)

Medvedev, Roy A. and Medvedev, Zhores A., *Khrushchev: The Years in Power* (Columbia University Press, 1976)

Nekrassow, Vladimir F, ed., *Berija. Henker in Stalin's Diensten. Ende einer Karriere* (Bechtermünz Verlag, 1997, in German)

Paloczi-Horvath, Georg, *Chruschtschow* (Fischer-Bücherei, 1961, in German)

Pistrak, Lazar, *The Grand Tactician. Khrushchev's Rise to Power* (Frederick A. Praeger, 1961)

Ponomarjow, Boris N., et al, *Geschichte der Kommunistischen Partei der Sowjetunion* (Dietz Verlag, 1973, in German)

Rapoport, Yakov, *The Doctors' Plot. Stalin's Last Crime* (Fourth Estate, 1991)

Resis, Albert, ed., *Molotov Remembers. Inside Kremlin Politics* (Ivan R. Dee, 1993)

Schwartz, Harry, *The Soviet Economy Since Stalin* (J. B. Lippincott Company, 1965)

Stalin, J., *Ökonomische Probleme des Sozialismus in der UdSSR* (Dietz Verlag, 1953, in German)

Talbott, Strobe, ed., *Chruschtschow erinnert sich. Die authentischen Memoiren* (Rowohlt, 1992, in German)

Taubman, William, *Khrushchev. The Man And His Era* (W. W. Norton & Company, 2003)

Webb, Sydney & Beatrix, *Soviet Communism: A New Civilisation*, Vol. 1 (Longmans, Green and Co., 1941)

Printed in the United States
By Bookmasters